GLOUCESTER

AND THE

CIVIL WAR

The 'Roundhead Association' of the English Civil War Society march to the relief of Gloucester! *(M. Atkin with thanks to Devereux's Regiment of the ECWS)*

GLOUCESTER

AND THE

CIVIL WAR

A CITY UNDER SIEGE

MALCOLM ATKIN AND WAYNE LAUGHLIN

ALAN SUTTON
in association with Gloucester City Museums

First published in the United Kingdom in 1992
Alan Sutton Publishing Ltd · Phoenix Mill · Far Thrupp · Stroud
Gloucestershire

First published in the United States of America in 1993
Alan Sutton Publishing Inc · Wolfeboro Falls · NH 03896–0848

British Library Cataloguing in Publication Data

Atkin, Malcolm
City Under Siege: Gloucester, 1643
I. Title II. Laughlin, Wayne
942.414062

ISBN 0 7509 0148 9

Library of Congress Cataloging in Publication Data applied for

*Cover illustration: The repair of the breach made in the south-east defences of
Gloucester during August 1643. Detail of original oil painting by W. Laughlin.*

Artist's impressions by Wayne Laughlin.

The royalties from this book have been donated to Gloucester City
Museums in order to further the study of Gloucester archaeology.

Typeset in 10/12 Garamond.
Typesetting and origination by
Alan Sutton Publishing Limited.
Printed in Great Britain by
The Bath Press, Bath, Avon.

Contents

List of Illustrations

MAPS

Foreword by the Sheriff of Gloucester

I was very pleased, as both Sheriff and Chairperson of the Leisure Services Committee, to be asked to write the preface for this important new study of Gloucester and the Civil War.

Those were momentous days for the development of government and society and the siege of Gloucester played an important role in determining the future of England. Yet today the evidence of the cannon that once thundered from the now so-elegant Gaudy Green has long been swept away. I hope that this book will help keep alive the history of those events – both as a reminder of the horrors of civil war and also as a testimony to the spirit of the people of Gloucester, united under adversity. It is a sobering fact to remember that if I had been Sheriff in 1642 or 1643 I would be preparing not just for council meetings, but also for war.

On a more cheerful note, the book has also reminded me, as Chairperson of Leisure Services, that one of the more positive aspects of the destruction caused by the siege was to encourage the creation of the first city amenity site. Apparently walks were created outside the South Gate to run down to the river – echoing our own twentieth-century efforts to promote what is now the Docks area of the city. My colleagues on the Planning Committee will also feel sympathy for their predecessors when they learn that such fine plans wre thwarted by someone building a noxious tannery on the same site.

Malcolm Atkin and Wayne Laughlin are both members of staff of the Leisure Services Department, working in the City Archaeology Unit. Their effort in taking the results of the painstaking archaeological work, setting it within its wider context of documentary and buildings research and in a form that can be appreciated and enjoyed by the local community

has been a real labour of love. I thank them and also Alan Sutton
Publishing Ltd for bearing the cost of the work.

I hope that you, the reader, will enjoy the book as much as I have. You
should also have the added satisfaction of knowing that by buying the
book you are providing funds to allow future archaeological projects in the
city to continue.

Jon Holmes
Gloucester Council Chamber
September 1992

Preface

Today, most people's impression of the Civil War is based on films, which set the conflict in a romantic or heroic light, and from seeing the painstakingly-accurate reconstructions of battles as performed by the English Civil War Society and the Sealed Knot. But amid the romance of the period we should not forget what the Civil War cost. No reconstruction can ever accurately portray the pain that war brought to the country. For the people of the time it was a devastating episode that tore local communities apart and set Englishman killing Englishman. Men, women and children fought and died in what now seem the most unlikely surroundings of Highnam, Brookthorpe and around the city itself on Southgate Street or in Barton. This is perhaps the most compelling reason for the people of Gloucester to, as the inscription commemorating the relief of the city over the South Gate exhorted, 'Ever Remember the Fifth of September'.

Acknowledgements

Thanks are owed to our colleagues A.P. Garrod, Philip Greatorex and Mark Walters for discussing the results of their unpublished watching briefs. Thanks also to Barbara Drake for her transcription of parts of the Corporation Accounts, to Andrew Saunders and Russell Howes for reading and commenting on earlier drafts, to Ian Barrett and Alan Turton of the English Civil War Society, and to Dennis Jay of Selwyn School. A special debt is owed to the late J.S. Whiting whose *Gloucester Besieged* has done much to popularize the accounts of the siege. A number of photographs are used through the courtesy of the British Library, Royal Armouries (Tower of London), Gloucestershire Records Office, Gloucester City Council and Andrew Saunders. Thanks also to the Director of Gloucester Museums Service (John Rhodes) for permission to illustrate finds from the collections. The help of the staff of the Gloucester Collection of Gloucestershire County Library Service and Gloucestershire Records Office is also gratefully acknowledged. A special thanks goes to Susanne Atkin for reading the text. Much of the detailed archaeological information derives from the excavations on Southgate Street and therefore it is appropriate to record our appreciation of the help provided by the Bank of England and Pearce Developments in funding that work. By the same token it is also important to note the commitment of Gloucester City Council in providing financial back-up for the excavations and particularly for funding the on-going programme of watching briefs across city and district.

Malcolm Atkin and Wayne Laughlin
Gloucester 1992

Introduction

We that had till that hour lived in great plenty and great order, found ourselves like fishes out of the water, and the scene so changed that we knew not at all how to act any part but obedience . . . we had perpetual discourse of losing or gaining towns and men; at the windows the sad spectacle of war, sometimes plague, sometimes sickness of other kinds . . .[1]

Until the outbreak of the Civil War in 1642, England had been spared the experience of war that ravaged much of Europe in the seventeenth century. But now all changed. This book attempts to give a flavour of what war meant to one town and district which, by its successful defence against the siege of 10 August–5 September 1643, has claim to being a deciding element in the eventual defeat of Charles I by the forces of Parliament. In its sterling defence we can also see, in the efforts of the local militia and town regiment, the spirit that was the inheritance of the Gloucestershire Regiment which was recruited forty-one years later in 1694.

For that fateful month during the summer of 1643 England's attention was focused on Gloucester. It was one year into the Civil War and King Charles had decided to besiege the city, after his success at the bloody siege of Bristol. It proved to be a fateful decision for, while King Charles I tried, unsuccessfully, to take the city, Parliament was able to regroup its forces and so ultimately to triumph in the war. News of the siege brought discussion of peace in London to an end and fostered a new determination to progress the war. The siege also established the reputation of Lt.-Col. Massey who was the military governor of Gloucester at the time – ironically resulting in him playing a major role in the restoration of Charles II. The reputation was well deserved as only about one-third of the sieges in the Civil War were successfully resisted.

The people of Gloucester had been preparing for war for some time but hurriedly built new defences even as an army of up to thirty thousand men

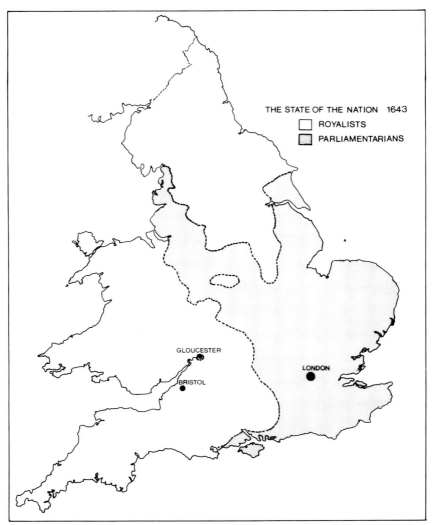

In August 1643 Gloucester was an isolated Parliamentary garrison in the heart of Royalist-held territory

arrived to bombard the city from above and try to mine it from below. The topography of the city and its legacy of surviving medieval buildings was irrevocably altered by the burning down of its suburbs. Yet today there are few reminders of these dramatic events. The defences of the Civil War lasted less than twenty years and were demolished at a time when the city was trying to live down its rebellious reputation.

The narrative of the siege has been well known since the republication of contemporary accounts in the nineteenth century. Both the main sources were written from the partisan viewpoint of the successful defenders. Indeed, we are dealing with a fascinating episode in the development of wartime propaganda. However, these accounts do not deal in any detail with the physical form of the defences. One of the authors was John Dorney, town clerk from 1641 to 1662 and again in 1667–74. His account (*A brief and exact relation of the . . . siege laid before the city of Gloucester*) was published within a month of the lifting of the siege on 22 September. An ardent anti-Royalist, he once declared 'Nothing had so much deceived the world as the name of a king.' His account is the most original and detailed, consisting of a day-by-day account of the siege. The other writer was John Corbet, son of a local shoemaker, the vicar of St Mary de Crypt and chaplain to Col. Massey. His *An historical relation of the military government of Gloucester* . . . was published in 1645 and in large part clearly borrows from Dorney. Although less precise in detail, his account includes much useful background comment. Also in 1643, Sergeant Henry Foster wrote an account of the march of the Earl of Essex's relief army, *A True and Exact relation of the Diurnall marching of the two regiments of the trained bands of the City of London*, which includes reminiscences of the siege as told to him by some of the inhabitants.[2] A much briefer, Royalist, account, *A Journal of the Siege of Gloucester*, was published in *Gloucestershire Notes and Queries* in 1887.[3] Little news of the siege appeared in the contemporary newsbooks but those references in the rival Parliamentary and Royalist publications offer contrasting opinions of events (many published in Fosbrooke, 1819). Some evidence of the financing of the war is contained in the Corporation Accounts and Minutes but there is also an interesting set of accounts by Thomas Blayney, Col. Massey's treasurer, which may represent the dealings of the more shadowy Committee for Defence.[4]

There are no contemporary plans of the defences or siegeworks, but a plan purporting to show the defences as an elaborate circuit of double ditches and bastions was plotted in 1780 (on what evidence it is not clear) in the Hall and Pinnell map. The first analysis of the proceedings was by J. Washbourn in 1825 and his collection of original source material from the period, published in *Bibliotheca Gloucestrensis*, remains invaluable. In 1860, the noted antiquary, Revd S. Lysons, drew up a plan showing the disposition of the Royalist forces and identifying the then-surviving earthworks beside the Hempsted Road.[5] Since that time, all physical trace of the defences has disappeared. Now, archaeology has provided a new source for study which provides a fresh insight into the physical effect that the war actually had on the city and on everyday life at that time.[6]

CHAPTER 1

Background to War

*This citty is not great but standeth holsomly and sweetly as it were upon a hill, the
streets descending every way from the Crosse*

JOHN SPEED

Seventeenth-century Gloucester, as described by John Speed and shown on
his plan of 1610, was still very much the medieval town of small, mainly
two-storey, houses cramped along the main streets and with large open
spaces around the margins. In 1640 the town had a population of about
four thousand five hundred with probably another five thousand living in
the surrounding district.[1] In all, Gloucester's authority covered *c.* 116.5 sq km
(45 square miles) including the Hundreds of King's Barton and Dudston
which extended as far as Norton, Badgworth, Witcombe, Brookthorpe,
Elmore, Highnam and Hartpury (see p. 63).

   The population was unevenly distributed within the city. The most expensive properties were in the centre of the city, west of The Cross in the parishes
of St Mary and All Saints. Landlords sought to exploit their investment in
these commercial areas to the maximum by subdividing buildings. Thomas
Pury (a clothier and alderman who will play a critical role in this story) sublet
two properties in Mercer's Alley off Westgate Street to be shared between two
haberdashers, a draper and a butcher. In 1627 one city centre shop 4 x $3^3/_4$ yd
was rented for £1 a year.[2] Houses cum shops had even been built along the
centre of Westgate Street during the medieval period and the row leading up
to The Cross consisted of a timber-framed range 26 m long, built four storeys
high including the attic.

   Away from this central area, the Speed plan of the city is a contrast
between further concentrations of housing – as on the north-west and
south margins, where some of the poorest lived – and open spaces that
were used for a variety of functions. The whole of the area between
Blackfriars gate (Q on Speed map) past the Castle to the Quay is shown as

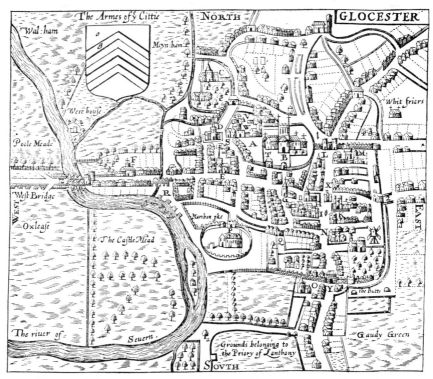

J. Speed's map of Gloucester, 1610. This gives a good impression of the city at the start of the Civil War. Most of the houses in the suburbs, outside the city walls, were destroyed at the start of the 1643 siege. This gives a good idea of what part of the medieval defences still survived at the start of the Civil War, and particularly the lack of defences on the north side of the city

being open land and included the fenced-off Maribon Park. The land adjacent to the river was used as docks for the port while other parts were simply a rubbish dump.[3]

The medieval walled town was surrounded by extensive suburbs spreading off the main approach roads on the north, east and south sides. By 1643 these contained up to one-third of the city's housing stock (over 240 houses). Here there was a stark contrast between the homes and workplaces of some of the poorest and some of the wealthiest of Gloucester society. The values of properties that were destroyed in the siege and listed in the Assessment of 1646 ranged from £10 to £300 and, for comparison, a single, *good* buff coat for an officer was valued at £10.

Around eight hundred houses were present in Gloucester at the time of the siege, yet only a few of the finer quality survive to the present day. Most of them date from the sixteenth century, and are timber-framed on stone footings with upper storeys projecting out on jetties. The latter provided more space and also served as a show of grandeur. Brick buildings were still rare and so special mention was made during the siege of 'the brick house' on the south-east corner of the defences. Notable surviving buildings from the late sixteenth century include the Folk Museum on Westgate Street (No. 101) and the remarkable four-storeyed No. 26 Westgate Street. The latter was traditionally thought to have been Col. Massey's headquarters during the siege, but this has now been discounted by modern research in favour of the Crown Inn, Westgate Street. Accounts survive which show the Corporation paying for the costs of Massey's accommodation at the Crown Inn to St Bartholomew's Hospital who owned the property.[4]

Gloucester Folk Museum on Westgate Street. This is one of the best-surviving examples of the better type of timber-framed house that was in Gloucester at the time of the siege. It was built in the sixteenth century

 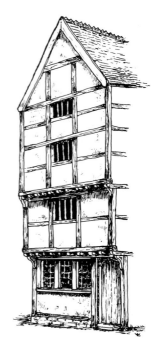

Left: No. 30 Westgate Street. One of the finest seventeenth-century houses in Gloucester, with the unusual feature of a double upper jetty. This was Mr Commeline's house at the time of the siege. It was hit by an incendiary shot during the night of Friday 25 August. *Right:* Reconstruction of seventeenth-century timber-framing to No. 30 Westgate Street (*after P. Moss*)

Surviving examples of seventeenth-century construction work include the rear block of No. 39 Westgate Street (beside Bull Lane) and the north range of No. 53 Westgate Street (The Fountain Inn). The most important survivor of this period is, however, No. 30 Westgate Street, which may date to about 1622. Built by the Corporation, it was first leased to the tailor, John Whithorne, but by 1640 had come into the hands of James Commeline, an apothecary of Dutch descent. It is an extremely exciting building in terms of Gloucester's building history, being one of the last purely timber-framed buildings to be erected; the roof still retains elements of medieval-type construction, and, peculiarly, the upper two floors are carried on a single jetty. The plan was of a single room on three floors with a kitchen at the rear. There was a back-to-back fireplace on the ground floor, serving the hall (later becoming the shop) and kitchen, with a bread oven beside it on the kitchen side, and fireplaces on each of the first and second floors (the third was unheated). Each upper floor originally had a garderobe (toilet) beside the staircase (and over the passage).[5] The building took a direct hit from red-hot shot during the siege on 25 August. Some of the roof timbers are, indeed, blackened but it is not possible to say whether this was from heat or simply through ageing. Other buildings of lesser quality may still lurk hidden behind eighteenth-century brick façades erected during a period in which the timber framing became unfashionable.

Surviving documentary evidence, such as wills, records the contents of some of the houses, but these documents generally represent only the wealthier elements in Gloucester society. With all classes, movable furniture and other goods were much sparser than we would expect today. This would possibly have made it easier for the inhabitants to clear out the houses that were to be demolished at the start of the siege.

The lives of the poorer majority of Gloucester society are largely undocumented, although the evidence of the later Hearth Tax returns

Sixteenth-century toilet (garderobe) on the first floor of Matson House, Gloucester. The chute is thought to have exited into a culvert running beside the house, and was therefore self-flushing. This was in the suite of rooms occupied by Charles I during the siege of 1643

suggests that one-quarter of Gloucester's population at the time may have been living on subsistence level (not in itself unusual for towns of the period). In 1672, 279 out of 1,028 households in Gloucester were excused the Hearth Tax and 401 had only one hearth.[6] Exemptions to the Hearth Tax, which imposed a charge of 2s 6d (12.5p) per hearth, were allowed for those not wealthy enough to pay the poor rate or not owning property valued at over £1 p.a. Perhaps 10 per cent of the population would have been poorly-paid servants and apprentices; many would have lived in the most basic conditions within what amounted to outhouses around the houses of the more wealthy, or in rooms within shared tenements.

Unfortunately the building levels of this period have been frequently destroyed in the city centre by subsequent clearance and cellarage, and the surviving archaeology is a very fragile resource indeed. Incomplete plans of poor quality tenements of the late sixteenth and seventeenth centuries were, however, excavated in 1972 at Nos 14–24 St Mary's Street, on the north edge of the city. The buildings, dated to the late sixteenth or early seventeenth century, consist of two unheated units, each probably of three rooms divided by a narrow passage. Following a movement of property boundaries, there was a change of plan and increase in comfort in the mid-seventeenth century with a single hearth added to each and one having an outbuilding added to the rear wall, but the rooms themselves may have got smaller. The floors were made of clay and the originally timber-framed walls sat on stone dwarf walls. The roofs would probably have been of stone tiles. Although there was no evidence from the excavation, it is likely that these dwellings were of two storeys.[7] Such houses would have been cold, damp and dingy, and took an inevitable toll on the health of the inhabitants, making them susceptible to a variety of infections and diseases.

Most houses and tenements had some form of organized, though primitive, sanitation by the seventeenth century. In the yards were open stone- or timber-lined cesspits in which cess and refuse could be rotted down before being periodically carted away to manure the surrounding fields or dumped in the river. Originally these pits were actually within buildings or attached to their rear walls, but by the seventeenth century their dangers to health were readily apparent and they had been moved out into the yard. The most elaborate seventeenth-century sanitary arrangement to have been excavated in the city was the vaulted stone-lined sewer running out of The Crown Inn on Westgate Street down to

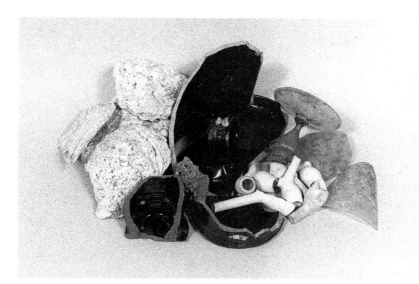

Finds, including drinking mugs, wine glasses, clay pipes (1640s–50s) and oyster shells, from the Civil War period sewer excavated in 1990 behind The Crown Inn, Westgate Street. Echoes of merriment in a puritan city? Colonel Massey lodged here during the siege. (*P. Greatorex for Gloucester City Museums*)

Quay Street. There were also a number of public lavatories – far more communal than we are used to today. One that remained in use from the fifteenth to mid-seventeenth century was a 'five-seater' which was excavated in 1989 at the junction of Southgate Street and the 'lost' street of St Owen's Lane leading to the now-destroyed St Owen's church. This was not a purely philanthropic gesture on behalf of the city – there was no drain to the latrine because the urine was a valuable commodity to be collected as an essential part of the dyeing and tanning industries.

Despite frequent attempts at regulation, much of the city's rubbish found its way out on to the street. Archaeological sections recorded outside St Nicholas's church on Westgate Street have highlighted the thick deposits of black organic rubbish that pass for the muddy tracks of the medieval and later streets – no better than the 'febly paved and full perilous and jepardous' surfaces of 1473.[8] An Act of 1641 condemned the condition of the streets and appointed days on which the citizens were to clean them (with a £12 fine for defaulters – a very substantial sum for the

An impression of life in a seventeenth-century suburb in Gloucester, based on archaeological evidence from excavations on St Mary's Street, Southgate Street and other finds

time). Animals freely roamed the streets – in 1572–3 a pound had to be made to hold the pigs that were caught wandering. Some advantage was taken of this during the Civil War when the soldiers from the garrison were allowed to kill and eat pigs that strayed on to the defences.[9]

One of the consequences of such rudimentary private sanitation was the danger to the water supply. There was a piped supply that came from Robinswood Hill into 'Scriven's Conduit' which was built in the middle of

Southgate Street during 1637 by Alderman Scriven (the conduit has been re-erected in Hillfield Gardens, Denmark Road). This supply was cut off during the siege of 1643, but much of the city's water probably still came from wells dug within the back yards or from public wells such as Trinity Well once lying in the middle of Westgate Street. These wells were easily contaminated from nearby cesspits, although those excavated on lower Southgate Street were deep (8 m) and the linings thickly sealed by clay to help prevent seepage from the sides. Not surprisingly, there were frequent outbreaks of 'plague'; that of 1603–5 killed one-tenth of the population of St Nicholas's parish.

Poverty and fatal and infectious diseases were an ever-present factor of life, and in this respect some in the city may have viewed the Civil War as merely another tragedy in their lives – albeit one entirely man-made.

Trade on the River Severn was still dominated by Bristol. But Gloucester's development as a port from the late sixteenth century acted as a spur to the merchants and retailers, the largest trade group in the early seventeenth century. The manufacturing of articles of dress was next in importance, but the local textile industry itself was in decline under com- petition from Cotswold villages (whose clothing industry was also com- plaining of the recession). In 1634, a weaver complained that there were now only six or seven looms in the city, whereas previously there had been over one hundred. The districts of the clothing industry across the country were major supporters of Parliament during the Civil War. The making of food and drink – particularly brewers and maltsters – was also important (Gloucester was a major centre of the grain trade), followed by the varied metalworking industries and tanning.[10] Unfortunately such industries do not leave many physical traces for posterity. The widespread textile industry, for example, may only be represented by a few fragments of the iron woolcombs. A lead bale seal from the East Gate excavations possibly reflects a consignment of French cloth or linen to the city. Pin-making was one of Gloucester's most famous post-medieval products and evidence of a seventeenth-century factory was discovered during the excavations on the East Gate in the form of large numbers of pins and unfinished wires.

Tanning was widespread in the north part of the city. The importance of the skin trade is illustrated in the Port Book of 1618–19 where calf skins with other products of the leather-working and tanning industries were among the strongest exports from the city. Two probably early seventeenth-century tanning workshops have been unearthed – one in the

Seventeenth-century pins and a 'pinner's bone' found on the 1988 excavations on the Bank of England site, Southgate Street. The 'pinner's bone' was a tool used to hold the pin steady while the tip was filed to a sharp point. (*P. Greatorex for Gloucester City Museums*)

rear range of a courtyard-plan building at No. 84 Northgate Street and the other within the medieval Tanners Hall. On both sites were found the rows of vats and troughs in which the hides were cleaned and cured in noxious mixtures of urine and animal droppings. A tannery treating smaller skins was built on the Southgate Gallery site in the immediate post-Civil War period (see p. 134).

Much of the industrial activity of the town still relied on agricultural products, and there was a strong connection between the town and the surrounding agricultural land which supplied it. In 1608, a number of the inhabitants living in the north and east wards of the city still worked on the land as 'husbandmen'. As a consequence, one of the main Royalist tactics during the war was to try to disrupt free movement between city and county.

The various types of pottery found in the city at this time provide a more tangible link with the everyday lifestyles of the inhabitants. They are mainly undecorated kitchen wares – jars and bowls – that were used for dry storage and baking. Pottery cooking vessels are rare, replaced during this period by metal vessels that have not survived. Also missing from the

Seventeenth-century pottery, including a 'bellarmine' imported from the Rhineland. Found in the backfill of the Civil War defences on Southgate Street. (*P. Greatorex for Gloucester City Museums*)

archaeological record are the treen (wooden) tableware that were only replaced by earthenware plates in the mid-seventeenth century. Most pottery from the period was brought from comparatively short distances with little that might be classed 'exotic' imports, although small quantities from further afield did come in from the Surrey–Hampshire border and Staffordshire. From the Rhineland came the ubiquitous stoneware jugs and mugs. Despite Gloucester's status as a port, the assemblages are more generally characteristic of those of an inland town rather than a trading settlement with extensive outside contacts.[11] The potteries were producing a greater range of items than previously, and this may reflect increasing sophistication in material possessions and living standards. But the survival of the pottery alone presents a distorted picture of the kitchen as an increasing proportion of the vessels would have been metal – cauldron, spit, jugs, pans and plates. These were longer-lasting, more adaptable and more valuable, and do in themselves reflect a greater wealth in the society. Unfortunately for the archaeologist they tended to be melted down for reuse rather than be thrown away.

In 1626 and 1628 the Corporation wrote to the Lord Lieutenant of the County pleading decay of trade due to plague, the decline of the cloth industry and migration of richer citizens as reasons for not being able to raise their normal contributions.[12] The economy did begin to slowly improve from the late 1620s so that, despite rises in prices, rent arrears on Corporation properties in 1641–2 were only £27, with the Corporation actually managing to balance the budget with a surplus of £18 1s $1/_4$d.[13] This was an age of contrasting fortunes. In a period of fixed incomes and rising prices some inhabitants were getting richer while others were getting poorer. The economic uncertainty was soon to turn some minds towards seeking more political solutions – and ultimately to war.

CHAPTER 2

Gloucester Takes Sides

That great God which is the searcher of my heart knows with what a sad sense I go upon this service, and with what a perfect hatred I detest this war without an enemy

LETTER OF SIR WILLIAM WALLER TO HIS FRIEND,
THE ROYALIST SIR RALPH HOPTON, 16 JUNE 1643

Gloucester was of great strategic importance in the English Civil War. The city controlled the south to north route to Worcester and Shrewsbury along the Severn, and the east to west road from London and Oxford into Wales. It was also of economic importance as a supply centre for both agricultural and manufacturing products – not least the timber and iron from the Forest of Dean.

The English Civil War truly was a conflict of 'A Nation Divided' and the complexities of loyalties go far beyond the popular stereotypes of 'Roundhead' and 'Cavalier'. When the Civil War formally broke out on 22 August 1642 most of the people of Gloucestershire, especially in the Severn Vale under the more direct influence of Gloucester, do appear to have taken the side of Parliament, with the main base of support being in what might now be loosely termed the 'middle classes' of yeomen, craftsmen, clothiers and traders whose aim was 'liberty and plenty' according to Corbet (or the 'most forward and seditious' to take the Royalist view of Clarendon). But the county was not united in this attitude. Even in Gloucester itself, the King's Secretary of State, Sir Edward Walker, was able to draw up a list in 1643 of 104 Royalist supporters (see p. 14). For many people the argument was less about any principle than self-preservation. Corbet tells how, after the fall of Bristol in July 1643, Gloucester

'. . . there were many well-affected people in the town'. Part of a list of 104 Royalist sympathizers compiled by King Charles's Secretary for State in 1643. (*British Library, Harley MSS, 1608, f.118, with permission*)

received deputations from some in the surrounding countryside calling for the city to surrender before the King sent his army into the region.

> The whole countrey forsook us . . . for they conceived the standing out of Gloucester, however advantageous to the Commonwealth, yet miserable for them; because by the falling down of a great army, they expected a destruction of corn and cattle, and if at last the King should not take in this place, to stoop perpetually under two burdens, and be cast into a remidilesse condition of misery and poverty.[1]

For these, a parliamentary victory would be hollow in leaving Gloucestershire as a battleground, whereas at least if the King won then the conflict would shift elsewhere. Charles I did indeed issue orders before the siege to 'seize the rents goods cattle and revenues of all delinquents

14

and persons ill affected to our Government within the said countie of Gloucester and the said countie of the citty of Gloucester'. But he justified this in order to free the city from 'untoward murders robberies rapines spoyles and oppressions . . . [carried out by the] Rebells now in Armes against us in the said cittie of Gloucester and in the countie of the same'.[2]

Corbet's isolationist view was probably exaggerated to make the victory of the city seem more dramatic. The Royalist Clarendon paints a very different picture of county loyalties towards Gloucester. He relates how, after the siege was raised, the inhabitants of the surrounding countryside

> as wonderful as any part of the story, caused all necessary provisions to be brought in to them, out of those very quarters in which the king's army had been sustained, and which they conceived to be entirely spent: so solicitous were the people to conceal what they had, and to reserve it for them.[3]

For as long as possible, the ordinary folk let the long-standing arguments of King and Parliament as to who should effectively rule the country pass over them – 'They care not what government they live under so as they may plough and go to market'.[4] For some, this attitude led eventually to the aggressive neutrality of the 'clubmen' who would fight whichever side tried to occupy their territory. Those of nearby Herefordshire and Worcestershire tacitly supported Parliament because it was the Royalist army that was occupying their region. But they would not take sides. Corbet called them 'foolish neuters' who had given 'assurance that they were our friends, but could not declare for either side'.[5] Col. Massey went further and wrote in 1645 that their rejection of his overtures to them was traitorous.[6] In Gloucestershire the tobacco growers of the Cheltenham and Winchcombe areas took arms against either side when they tried to prevent the planting of new crops and many in the Forest of Dean were driven to banditry as their livelihoods were disrupted by both armies.

SOCIAL DIVISIONS – AND UNITIES

Economics and religion combined to create a new intensity of political awareness and all classes were split by the issues. In Gloucestershire the wealthy Cotswolds landowner and JP, Nathaniel Stephens of Chavenage, had been imprisoned in 1636 over his refusal to pay Ship Money and was also prosecuted in the Court of Star Chamber for his obstruction of the new restrictive cloth laws. In June 1641 he presented a petition on behalf of the Forest of Dean against the Catholic Sir John Wyntour for transporting arms – reflecting the current fears of a papist plot. He was one of a small number of gentry, including Sir Robert Cooke of Highnam, who (along with city alderman Thomas Pury) were exempted from the King's pardon to Gloucester in 1642 and remained leaders of the parliamentary cause in Gloucestershire. On 25 August 1642 it was Nathaniel Stephens, along with his brother Edward and Sir Robert Cooke, who called a meeting to try to unite the gentry on Parliament's side. Others included Sir John Seamore and Thomas Hodges of Shipton Moyne (who also features prominently in Gloucester Council business throughout the war). Together, they made arrangements for the rendezvous of the militia, volunteers and troops of horse 'upon all alarms'.[7]

These gentry were the exceptions. Corbet described the Gloucestershire Royalists as essentially being the 'powerful gentry' who were guilty of 'deserting their country either by open emnity or detestable neutrality' because of their hatred of the Commons, religion and a self interest in wishing to protect their estates against possible seizure by the King.[8] Thirty-three were included in a draft order of 1643 from the King calling on local gentry to raise forces against Gloucester.[9] A total of sixty-one members of the local gentry who had supported the King were later fined in return for being allowed to keep their estates.[10] For some, the decision to support the King would have been difficult. Like Nathaniel Stephens, John 'Crump' Dutton had refused to collect the Ship Money and had been imprisoned earlier for refusing to pay the 'forced loan' for the war with France and Spain in 1625, but ultimately he believed that his loyalty lay with his king. Like Dutton, most of the Royalist gentry came from the Cotswolds – men such as Lord Chandos of Sudeley, who was Lord Lieutenant of the county from 1641, and achieved fame at the battle of Newbury by having three horses killed under him, Sir Robert Poyntz from Acton Court, who wrote a vindication of the monarchy, and Viscount Tracy of Toddington. Tracy was later held at Gloucester as a 'delinquent' while his son Robert was a royal commissioner during the period of the siege. From the Forest of Dean came Sir John Wyntour, Sir Baynham Throgmorton of Clearwell and the Colchester family of Westbury. In the event, a good deal of the military action in the county focused on capturing and recapturing their country houses so that 'every corner of the county is pestered with garrisons'.[11] This inevitably caused considerable disruption and destruction. Lord Chandos's Sudeley changed hands three times during the war and in 1646 the garrison was ordered to stop using the fine panelling for firewood. This was all to little avail as the building was slighted in 1648–50. There were similar stories from the opposing side. The manor house of the Stephens's family at Lypiatt Park was burnt down by Royalist troops in 1645 while evicting a parliamentary garrison. Sir John Wyntour burnt down his own house, 'White Cross' at Lydney, in 1645 so as to stop it falling into Massey's hands.

The tendency of the local gentry to support the King meant that the local parliamentary forces were deprived of the 'natural' officers of the day. In early 1643 Corbet described how the defence of the county rested with the poorly-trained volunteers 'which were yet as a cake not turned, a kinde of souldiers not wholly drawn off from the plow or domesticke imployments'.[12] He had no sympathy in those cases where the common folk could be shown to have supported the King, dismissing them with characteristic xenophobia as coming from 'blinde Wales, and other dark corners of the land'![13]

The conflict produced strange bedfellows and many establishment figures in the parliamentary side were uneasy as to the dangers of encouraging a strength of popular feeling that might lead to a questioning of the structure of society itself. After Lord Chandos was attacked at Cirencester in September 1642 Corbet commented on the fury of the common people that 'prudent men promote and maintaine, yet no farther than themselves can over-rule and moderate'.[14] Like Dorney he bemoaned the fact that resistance was left to a 'rash and confused multitude', deprived of their traditional leaders.[15] Other commoners were equally capable of taking action into their own hands. In September 1643 the villagers around Berkeley Castle attacked patrols sent out by the Royalist governor of the castle. Tenants on county estates acted with less high ideals as the mounting chaos offered an opportunity to refuse to pay rent and settle old grudges. Parliament later had to face the consequences of this social disorder. In 1650 a 'rude multitude' tore down fences on local estates around Frampton and Slimbridge and had to be quelled by a troop of cavalry.[16]

How had this situation arisen?

ECONOMICS

A number of general complaints contributed to the widespread atmosphere of mistrust that led to eventual rebellion, although they cannot be taken as reasons in themselves for determining a region's loyalties. The Crown was financially weak and had been driven to rely on a number of extraordinary forced loans and taxes that were imposed without parliamentary consent. Local merchants would have been hit by the levy of 'tonnage and poundage' (duties on imports and exports). But above all, people objected to the Ship Money Tax (intended to pay for a refurbishment of the fleet), which was extended throughout the country in 1635 and affected virtually anyone who had any possible means to contribute. It was extended by 'Coat and Conduct' money in 1639 to pay for the army's campaign in Scotland. Gloucestershire only collected 2 per cent of the £5,500 due from Ship Money in 1640 and the tax was eventually abolished in 1641. There was a similarly poor response in collecting the 'Coat and Conduct' money. Opposition at one level was simply against what was considered unfair and excessive taxation during a time of economic uncertainties. But the imposition of taxes without the consent of Parliament during the eleven years of 'personal rule' from 1629–40 was also feared as a signal of the absolutist ambitions of Charles I in wanting to rule completely without Parliament.

LOCAL CONCERNS

But such general concerns affected areas that remained loyal to the King. Of more special concern to Gloucestershire were the restrictions on the clothing industry and attacks on the local tobacco-growing industry.

The local clothier interests, as nationally, saw their industry in decline and placed under increasing control from London. It is significant that one of the principal moving forces behind Gloucester's stand was the clothier Thomas Pury, while the landowner Nathaniel Stephens also saw his interests allied with the local industry. Sir Arthur Aston wrote from Painswick to Prince Rupert during the lead-in to the siege on 7 August that 'indeed there is scarcely one of all these clothiers but have both lent money, and do maintain soldiers upon their own charges against . . . his majesty'.[17]

The tobacco-growing industry enjoyed a brief period of importance in the county during the seventeenth century as the centre of English

Foresters tear down Sir John Wyntour's enclosure fences to protect their livelihood. Local antagonisms could shape the wider loyalties of a region

production of the crop and involved around six hundred growers in the Cheltenham and Winchcombe areas. Charles I had sought to abolish the industry in order to protect the higher price of tobacco imported from the Virginia tobacco plantations. This naturally caused resentment against the Royalist government of the day and therefore led to initial support for the parliamentary cause. In 1636 there were threats of violence from Gloucestershire towns against any who tried to interfere with production, and violent riots occurred in succeeding years. The planters took advantage of the confusion of the war years to pursue their trade in peace, but afterwards, the Commonwealth followed exactly the same policy as their Royalist predecessors and the loyalties of the planters then reversed.

The Forest of Dean had its own particular strategic importance for its supply of timber and iron – both vital for the war effort of either side. The Forest had no particular tendency to national causes either way at the start of the Civil War and most local people probably tried to affect a neutrality for as long as possible, despite skirmishes as at Coleford in February 1643 where the garrison of Col. Burrowes was assisted by local people – a 'rabble of the common people' according to Clarendon – against the Catholic Lord Herbert's advancing army. During the fighting, the market house was burnt down and a sniper killed Herbert's commander of foot, Col. Lawly. The Foresters' attitude had undoubtedly been affected by the virtual sale for £106,000 and a yearly rent of £1,950 12s 8d, in 1640, of the Forest (including wood, coppices, waste, mines and quarries) to the Catholic and firm Royalist, Sir John Wyntour (he was the Queen's secretary and cousin to Lord Herbert). He aroused considerable local bitterness, not necessarily for his religion or for his Royalist sympathies, but more importantly because his economic policies of enclosures and felling threatened local livelihoods. The Foresters tore down the enclosure fences at night and declared 'that so often as the said enclosures shall be repaired, they will do the like, and turn in their cattle as they were wont to do before the said improvement'.[18] Later events were to show that they, as with the men of Frampton and Slimbridge, were as ready to do this under the Commonwealth as they were under Charles I.

Wyntour was campaigning in 1645 in the Forest with a force of over three thousand five hundred men, but these were troops loaned from elsewhere. It is not clear how many he managed to recruit locally, other than from his own household. Although he received the King's summons to support the siege at Gloucester in 1643 he kept a low profile until afterwards, but then his fortified house at Lydney ('White Cross') became the principal base of Royalist operations in the area. Corbet accused Wyntour of pretending 'innocency till his hour was come' but then being 'a plague of the Forest and a goad in the sides of the garrison' (of Gloucester).[19] It is a sign of the times that his cousin, Col. Charles Wyntour, was captured at Coleford in February 1643, fighting alongside the townsfolk on the parliamentary side. An example of local feeling from the Welsh side of the Forest came in March 1644 when Thomas Dabridgecourt wrote to Prince Rupert begging the latter 'I will go on my bare feet to serve you, but from the Welsh, good lord deliver me'. In complaining about the lukewarm loyalty of the Monmouthshire folk for the Royalists he went on to say 'They value neither Sir John Winter, his warrants, nor mine, nor any'.[20] In 1645 Prince Rupert certainly treated the Forest as hostile territory as he twice ravaged the area, driving some locals into the mines for shelter and actually inspiring others to take up arms – either as bandits or mercenaries. By contrast, the parliamentary side thought that they would have better success in trying actively to recruit the Foresters. In September 1644, John Barrough (?Burrowes) was ordered to raise a regiment of foot from the Forest of Dean.[21] Colonel Edward Harvey tried the same in October of that year but both efforts seem to have been frustrated through lack of money.

PURITANISM

> . . . he would never more trust any man that wore his hair shorter than his ears . . .
>
> (John Dutton, Royalist MP for Gloucestershire)

The focus of the niggling grievances against the King became religion. The latter played a central part in the life of the country and could arouse immense passions. The strong local tradition of puritanism extending back into the sixteenth century originally developed as a movement to 'purify' the existing Church of England. Opponents saw it as dour and dismal. In 1618 the maypole in Gloucester's St Nicholas's parish was taken down but this is not to say that the 'civil, courteous and religious'[22] inhabitants of seventeenth-century Gloucester were paragons of virtue.

A 'Puritan' church. Taynton church, lying between Gloucester and the Forest of Dean, was built in 1647 after its predecessor had been burnt down during a skirmish. It followed the puritan fashion of a north to south alignment and originally consisted only of a hall-like nave. The chancel was added subsequently. Outside the church on the east side is a monument to Thomas Pury the younger, one of the captains in the Town Regiment of Gloucester during the siege (d. 1693)

'Tippling' and the unauthorized selling of beer increased substantially during the war years – no doubt spurred by the presence of the garrison.

By the 1630s several lectureships had been created to provide a ministry based on preaching from the Bible as an alternative to the established church and its increasing emphasis on ritual. In 1633 the Gloucester lecturer John Workman was tried by the Church Court of High Commission for preaching against images, dancing and allegedly calling for the election of ministers. The preaching movement was supported by the City Council who in 1641 petitioned Parliament that eight poor parishes should be united in order to provide a teaching ministry. This brought them into conflict with Archbishop Laud, who had become a symbol nationally of the trend towards 'High Church', but had sown the seeds of his unpopularity in Gloucester much earlier. As Dean of Gloucester Cathedral from 1616–21, Laud had caused much local resentment by his movement of the Communion Table to form a railed-off altar at the east end – seen as a sign of the separation of the congregation from the ritual of the clergy. (The fine Jacobean altar rails still survive in the Lady Chapel.) The outraged Bishop, Miles Smith, is said never to have entered the Cathedral again! His successor, Bishop Geoffrey Goodman, was more amenable and was imprisoned in 1640 for refusing to denounce Catholic practices.

The Puritan emphasis on discipline and order appealed to the Council's desire to improve public services in an attempt to fend off possible disorder from the poorer classes of society. Thus the rise in what was seen as extravagant ritual within the Church and the King's insatiable demands for money brought the careful administrators of the city into natural conflict with central government. The City Council sought to confirm their powers over the hospitals and Crypt School which Laud rejected as interfering in Church prerogative.[23] The city petitioned Parliament in September 1641 against the need for an episcopacy, and one of the city's MPs from 1640, the radical Alderman Thomas Pury, took part in the debates over the 'Root and Branch' Bill in June 1641, calling for the 'utter eradication of Bishops, Deans and Chapters'.[24] Pury was described by a Royalist at the time of his election in 1640 as 'once a weaver, now an attorney, whom I think, nothing has so much endeared as his irreverence in God's house, sitting covered when all the rest sit bare'. He was also described as a man who 'bears no goodwill to gentlemen' by Thomas Tracy in August 1644, writing to Col. Harvey in London to intercede for his aged father, John

Viscount Tracy of Toddington, held in Gloucester as a 'delinquent', appealing not as Royalist to Parliamentarian but as two members of the same gentry class.[25] Puritan feelings were further inflamed by the revolt of the Ulster Catholics in October 1641 and the massacre of Protestants there which heightened the fear of Catholic plots against a reformed Church of England. As King Charles tried to raise an army to quell the rebellion, the fears as to whether he could be trusted with an army – which might ultimately be used against the English Parliament – intensified.

Religious fervour had also reached the army. In 1640 a captain from the Gloucestershire levies called to fight in the war with the Scots complained that the Puritans 'had strongly possessed the soldiers that all the commanders of our regiments were Papists, so I was forced for two or three days to sing psalms all the day I marched, for all their religion lies in a psalm'.[26] It was a real threat: some officers were actually executed for suspected Catholic sympathies during this campaign.

For most of those involved, opposition to the King was not a rebellious stance. They saw themselves as 'protecting' the existing parliamentary status quo, under threat from the King and his advisers, and their Protestant religion from a fear of Catholic conspiracy. The threat seemed very real. In Gloucester on 4 June 1641 there were reports to Parliament of two loads of armour which were to be hidden in a 'Papist's' (the term used for Catholics at the time) house near Gloucester. In defence of the state, the militia were later instructed to make a search of suspected places and disarm 'Papists' and ill-affected clergy.[27]

Even to the start of the siege of Gloucester in 1643 – if only as a convention – the citizens professed their loyalty to the King – but only as he acted through Parliament. The mayor at the time of the siege, Dennis Webb, was particularly concerned over his existing oath of allegiance when the King himself demanded the city – despite the fact that he had been one of the leaders of the attack on the Welsh forces at Highnam in March 1643. The city's reply to the King's summons to surrender was delayed 'after some debate in satisfying Mr Mayor's scruples touching his oath of majorality'.[28]

CHAPTER 3

The Outbreak of War

GLOUCESTER'S DEFENCES FIRST TESTED

Gloucestershire very quickly established its allegiances in the war. When Lord Chandos tried to execute the Commission of Array (to take control of the local militia for the King) in Cirencester in August 1642 a mob set upon him. On 1 September Mr Hill, the under-sheriff of Gloucester, with ten men set upon Sir Ralph Dutton and ten Royalists who were trying to raise more men for the King.[1] On 10 September Sir John Byron set out from Oxford to join the King's army with a troop of horse and 'divers scholars volunteers' but they were attacked by 'the country' at Stow-on-the-Wold and lost ten men. The first major action that the Gloucester forces were involved in was also in September. One hundred and fifty men from Gloucester's 'Trained Bands' (the local militia), under the command of Captain Scriven (son of the ironmonger John Scriven who had been mayor of Gloucester in 1641) were sent to assist Col. Fiennes in attempting to seize Worcester and were involved in a 'hot skirmish' there. Fiennes was defeated by Prince Rupert's cavalry at Powick Bridge (in the modern county of Hereford and Worcester) on 22 September.

Corbet was scathing in his assessment of the worth of the Trained Bands of the time as although providing 'the main support of the realm and its bulwark against unexpected invasion, [they] were effeminate in courage and incapable of discipline, because their whole course of life was alienated from warlike employment'.[2] They were organized into companies under local captains but Parliament was able to send down training officers to improve their quality. In Gloucester they had been supplemented by a company of Volunteers raised in July 1642. The strategic position of Gloucester meant that it could not be ignored for long. Measures for improving the defences of the city had started before the actual declaration

Key:
- Site of garrison
- - - March of King Charles to Gloucester and his retreat
- - - - March of Essex to relieve Gloucester
- .... Return march of Essex
- Mythe Site of skirmish or battle

| 0 | 5 | 10 | 15 | 20 km |
| 5 | | 10 | 12 | miles |

... every corner of the county is pestered with garrisons'. Civil War garrisons and skirmishes in Gloucestershire

of war on 22 August 1642. Initial responsibility for constructing and financing the defence works was put into the hands of a special 'Committee for Defence' rather than being organized by the City Council.[3] Both were distinct from the military command in Gloucester which was not established until November. The Earl of Essex was appointed as the first governor, replaced in December by the Earl of Stamford. Stamford quickly moved on to Bristol and left the 23-year-old Lt.-Col. Edward Massey in charge as deputy governor with a regiment of troops.

The King needed to clear the route into the Royalist areas of South Wales to allow his troops to move freely eastwards. Cirencester was the first obstacle to this but was captured by Prince Rupert on 2 February 1643. The next day Prince Rupert called upon Gloucester to surrender, but Massey and his officers replied 'that they were resolved with their lives and fortunes to defend the city for the use of the king and parliament, and in no wise would surrender at the demand of a forraigne prince'.[4]

This emphasis on not surrendering to a foreign prince was later to give hope to King Charles that the city would surrender to him in person. The threat to Gloucester was acute and 'the hearts of many sunke very low and began to lye flat . . .'.[5] Drastic measures were called for and it was decided to sacrifice Sudeley and Tewkesbury whose garrisons were withdrawn to strengthen that of Gloucester, by 200 foot and further dragoons (mounted infantry).[6]

Much to the city's relief, Prince Rupert did not press his claim on Gloucester and withdrew to Cirencester. Stories were fabricated by parliamentary newspapers in London (but, significantly, not reported locally) in order to maintain morale. They claimed that Prince Rupert actually launched an attack on Gloucester in February – having been fooled into believing that some of the city gunners would defect and so only fire above the heads of the charging Royalists. The graphic, but probably fictitious, reports tell how the gunners did indeed set the first volley above the heads of the attacking Royalists – but only as part of a deception to draw them into a trap, whereupon they unleashed some hidden cannon and killed many men.[7]

The noose did seem to be around Gloucester's neck. Throughout the month of February there were complaints that Prince Rupert was looting the county and had sent back 200 cartloads of plunder to the King's headquarters in Oxford. Prince Rupert tried to levy monthly taxes on the villages and towns of the county, claiming £3,000 to establish the new

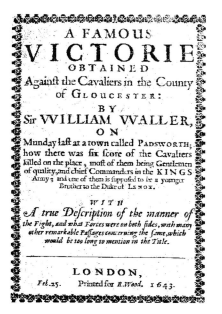

A FAMOUS
VICTORIE
OBTAINED
Against the Cavaliers in the County
of GLOUCESTER:
BY
Sir WILLIAM WALLER,
ON
Munday laſt at a town called PADSWORTH;
how there was ſix ſcore of the Cavaliers
killed on the place, moſt of them being Gentlemen
of quality, and chief Commanders in the KINGS
Army; and one of them is ſuppoſed to be a younger
Brother to the Duke of LENOX.

WITH
A true Deſcription of the manner of
the Fight, and what Forces were on both ſides, with many
other remarkable Paſſages concerning the ſame, which
would be too long to mention in the Title.

LONDON,
Feb. 25.   Printed for R. Wood. 1643.

Newssheet describing Waller's victory at
Padworth (?Badgworth), February 1643.
(*Gloucester Collection, Gloucester City Library,
with permission*)

garrison at Cirencester and a further £4,000 per month to maintain it.[8] According to the parliamentary *Perfect Diurnal* these villages 'bravely resisted his summons, and stood their guard, which he perceiving, left them, without any further attempt'. The town of 'Padsworth' (?Badgworth) rallied 300 men to beat off a Royalist assault (killing 100 according to their account) but then decided to abandon the place and took their goods to Gloucester.[9] Waller was also in action there on 20 February. He was warned of an approach of 1,600 Royalists and, realizing that he was outnumbered, drew up his men in a 'battalia' to fire two volleys (the reference to 'charging' is to loading muskets) apparently before the enemy could reply – 120 Royalists in all were killed. A pamphlet published on 25 February gives a graphic description of the scene.

> He caused all his men to stand in a battalia and discharge upon the enemy at once, upon the word given, which being done, at the first onset of the enemy there was about 80 of them slain, which slaughter on a sudden put them in such a fright, that they presently retreated back, and before they could be brought up again Sir William

Waller's men had charged the second time, and gave them the same entertainment as they had before, killing 40 more.[10]

Waller was an inventive general. On 10 March 1643 it was reported that he had sent out notices pretending to originate from Prince Rupert

to give the people notice, that stood affected to the king, that Prince Rupert did require them to bring in their horses and other provisions to such a place by a day certain, at which time his highnesse will be there, & which the malignants of the county obeyed with cheerfulness; by which policy Sir William Waller got some of their best horses.[11]

But the Royalist noose was tightening further. An entry of 6 March in the Gloucester Council Minute Books orders in provisions because 'this city is threatened with a siege'.[12] While Royalist forces under Prince Maurice were harrying the city on the north and east, pressure was

Part of the Royalist earthworks dug at Highnam in March 1643. According to the Journal of Sir Samuel Luke, these were supposed to have been levelled after the city victory. Scale in half metres

also increasing from the west as Lord Herbert's Welsh army of 1,500 foot and 500 horse (under Sir Jerome Brett) advanced through the Forest of Dean and encamped at Highnam, 2 miles (3.2 km) from the city. Here they dug in (parts of the ditch still survive next to the church) in order to command the roads into the Forest and Newent (modern A40 and A48), but still did not attempt any direct assault on the city. King Charles also tried economic sanctions, ordering that because the city

> had so obstinately stood out against his authority . . . none of his other subjects of this county should have any trade, traffick, or commerce with them until they should return to their former duty.[13]

As in a chess game, Massey planted forces to check Brett in the recently fortified former Bishop's Palace at Over. So they remained, in 'a stinking nest' according to Corbet, for a month with little evidence of action, evidently hoping for the support of Prince Rupert's army. The temporary support of 250 cavalry and dragoons from Bristol allowed the city to take a more active role in mounting sallies and harrying the Royalists, during which period 'our blew regiment became a terrour to those miserable Welch-men'. These were probably men of the Trained Bands of whom Corbet had been so disparaging earlier, and were commanded here by Dennis Wise. The latter, a lawyer by profession, was mayor and apparently had taken readily to arms, being described as 'a sword-man as well as a gown man'.[14]

In a dramatic twist of fortune, Massey and Sir William Waller were then able to execute a daring plan that destroyed the Welsh 'mushroom' army and gave the city a much-needed respite. Sir William Waller had been campaigning in Wiltshire and convinced the Royalists that his interest was still in the east of Gloucestershire by carrying out a feint towards Cirencester. The 'Night Owl' then ordered a rapid forced march overnight to Frampton Passage on the River Severn where a bridge of boats supplied by Massey was waiting for him. He then got undetected behind the Welsh army in the Forest of Dean and camped on the night of 23 March at Huntley, 5 miles to the west of Highnam. Massey kept the Welsh busy during the day and ensured that no spies got out at night so that they were unaware of the force that had gathered in their rear. Massey attacked the next day in order to draw the Welsh out against what they thought were outnumbered forces – then Waller appeared from behind with a

Fleeing Welsh troops are cut down at Barber's Bridge by troopers from Gloucester

warning shot and drew up his troops to suggest that he had got a far larger force than indeed he had. This clearly created a panic and the city troops were able to storm a redoubt. It was then agreed to parley over possible terms of surrender for the Welshmen. The outraged Royalist newsbook *Mercurius Aulicus* accused Waller of 'perfidiousness and treachery' by launching a final assault during this time, but Corbet asserts that the Welsh simply remained within their fortifications and refused to try to slip away under cover of night, surrendering without a struggle the next morning (25 March).

The parliamentary forces killed 500 men and took as prisoners 1,442 'common soldiers', and 150 'gentlemen' said to have included 'many of the chief of Wales and Herefordshire'.[15] Eighty-six bodies were found buried in a hillock in the nineteenth century, lying beside the scene of the battle at Barber's Bridge, beyond Rudford (on the road from Highnam to Newent), where the parliamentary forces caught up with the Welshmen during one of the skirmishes. An unknown number of bodies were also found when cutting the nearby canal in the 1790s. Of perhaps more practical value to the city, the parliamentarians also seized 1,600 weapons, 4 cannon and other provisions; these were to prove very useful later. Massey destroyed Highnam House itself – despite it being the home of his ally, Sir Robert Cooke.

The prisoners seized at Highnam were held in St Mary de Lode and Holy Trinity (in the middle of Westgate Street). One of the prisoners, 'Welsh Thomas' from Carmarthen, was only sixteen or seventeen years old when he was captured. He described in 1717 how he was fed on 'turnip tops, cabbage leaves or any such things'. In all only £18 19s was spent on bread to distribute to the private soldiers. The discovery from within the church of numbers of clay pipes of the period that have non-local markings does, however, suggest that they may have had tobacco – at least for a while.[16] Even with this paltry level of care such a large number of prisoners were a burden on the city, but they were also a potential security risk. After ten days most were released – after the usual promises had been made that they would not fight against Parliament again. For many this was merely a token gesture; certainly 'Welsh Thomas' later fought in the siege itself.[17]

Pressure on the city was then further relieved by Massey and Waller retaking Tewkesbury on 12 April and seizing Hereford on 30 April. New troops were raised and trained. In April, Henry Stephens raised a Town

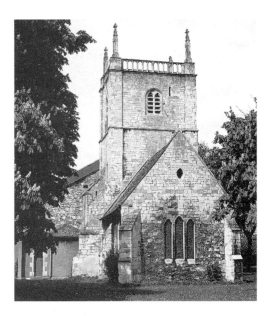

St Mary de Lode church, Gloucester. This was used as a prison for the Welsh troops captured at Highnam. There they were fed on 'turnip tops, cabbage leaves or any such things'

Regiment for Gloucester, possibly out of the nucleus of the Trained Bands and Volunteer company (unfortunately Stephens himself was captured on 23 June at Oddington, near Stow, leaving command to Massey as the 'Governor's Regiment'). The regiment was supplied with some items of equipment (thirty swords and baldricks to a cost of £10) out of a public collection in Gloucester in August.[18]

It was a period of great ups and downs for the region as the opposing forces jockeyed for position, but what appeared to be a fatal disaster to the parliamentary cause came with the three-day siege and fall of Bristol from 23 to 26 July. Corbet described how 'That sudden surrender . . . which was almost beyond our feares, brought forth a dark gloomy day to the city of Gloucester'.[19] This freed the Royalist army to be able to march on either London or Gloucester. Thus was the city about to experience one of the most dramatic events in its long history.

ORGANIZED FOR WAR

How could the city possibly resist an army that had conquered Bristol in only three days? The Speed map of 1610 gives a good impression of the

A great deal of the armour used in the first years of the Civil War were archaic pieces, as with these late sixteeenth-century types of burgonet and morion. Found at Brookthorpe. (*P. Greatorex for Gloucester City Museums*)

nature of Gloucester's defences as they existed prior to the outbreak of the war. They had long been more of an economic barrier and status symbol rather than having a military significance and it was a frequent complaint of medieval kings that the citizens only took notice of their defences in a time of actual crisis. Ironically as it turned out, it was Charles I who had ordered the latest restoration of the defences. On 16 September 1640 (during the 'Bishop's Wars' with Scotland) the King's Council of State instructed the Lord Lieutenant of Gloucestershire to ready

> a sufficient number of able pioneers, good carts furnished with men and horses, and a sufficient number of spades, shovels, pickaxes and other tools necessary for the making of works for defence in these perilous times.[20]

By 1642 and the outbreak of the Civil War, the existing medieval walls had become so dilapidated that the section adjacent to the North Gate had actually fallen down in 1641 and trees were allowed to grow in the ditch.[21]

Corbet described Gloucester at the start of the Civil War as being 'open on three parts at least, and had no considerable defence'.[22] These medieval defences were, in any case, designed to counter a very different type of warfare than the artillery barrages to be expected in the seventeenth century.

As early as February 1642 the Corporation had ordered the purchase of forty muskets and bandoliers from London and twenty of the same from Bristol for the Trained Bands.[23] As tension mounted, the 'Gloucester Volunteers' were founded by July 1642. A 'Committee for Defence' for the city was set up on 5 August 1642 and the deputy lieutenants for the city were instructed to 'raise whatever fortifications should be thought fit, for the preservation of the city'. As part of this, 'seaven severall iron chaynes well and sufficiently made and provided for the seaven severall gates of this city' were bought to string across the approach roads as well as 'ten severall turned picks well bound and fitted with iron to be placed at such lanes and places that shalbe thought fitt that lye most open for horse or foote to enter, to prevent such theyr entrance'. The 'turned picks' (turnpikes) were settings of pikes which were the seventeenth-century equivalent of modern tank traps to hinder cavalry charges. Over two hundred pikes for this purpose were bought before the siege (see Appendix 3). Of particular interest is the reference to 'twenty or thirty pickaxes and twenty or thirty spades and shovells and some ten or twelve wheele barrows presently provided to helpe to make barracadoes by digging of ditches to prevent horses entrance into the city'.[24] It was also decided to purchase three or four cannon. In all the Corporation spent £198 2s 5d on arms, ammunition and fortifications in 1642.[25] Most of the money was raised by a levy on members of the Common Council. In January 1643 Parliament set aside a further £500 as payment for the expenses 'laid out upon the fortifications and other provisions' for the defence of Gloucester.[26]

Thus, much of the framework for the defences may well have been established before the arrival of Massey (who was an experienced engineer officer – see Appendix 2), with the initial work possibly directed by Samuel Baldwin, a local mason and later described by Dorney as the 'surveyor of the defences' during the siege period. Apart from the cost of the defences, there was also the cost of maintaining the garrison. The Corporation tried to limit its direct financial responsibilities and keep defence expenditure (the responsibility of the Committee for Defence) distinct from its normal affairs but was, nevertheless, forced to take out loans to cover the costs of keeping the troops that it expected Parliament

'All suspended private care, and the women and children acted their parts in making up the defects of the fortifications.' The excavation of the earthworks around the city was a massive community undertaking. Digging the 4 m deep and 10 m wide defences outside the South Gate, 1643

ultimately to cover. If they had not, the consequences would have been dire, for the troops were described in March 1643 as being 'mutinous and desperate', held together only by Massey's skill.[27] Corbet gives the reasons that

> no monies came from the state, and but small supplies out of the country, that the vilest mutineers were to be dealt with by entreaty, their insolences to be suffered with patience . . . the city was constrained to free quarter and great disbursements by way of loane.[28]

Although £1,000 was held in London for the pay of the garrison from November 1642, it was not actually received by the city until October 1644.[29] In the mean time the city had to arrange loans and even sell its civic plate to pay the troops.[30] The problem was compounded by the fact that citizens were expected to provide quarters – 'freequarter' – for the garrison from February to June 1643 at the rate of 3s per man.[31] Aldermen had to accommodate six men, councillors four men and the rest of the population in proportion.[32] The wealthy could afford to pay for others to take on this responsibility, but thereby increased the burden on the poorer sections of the community. A special order was given requiring the quartering of the reinforcements that came in March.[33] In that month Mrs Hayward who lived in the north suburb had to quarter three soldiers for a month.[34] She was of only modest means and her house (soon to be destroyed in the siege) was valued at only £10. Ultimately, repayment was made over one year later (September/October 1644) and then only at the flat rate of 4s 6d in the pound. This indicates that over £4,000 was spent by the inhabitants in housing the garrison during that five-month period before the siege.[35] But the citizens of Gloucester faced a double burden, for as well as freequarter they were also expected to contribute towards the soldiers' pay in the form of weekly assessments, other loans and collections. Not surprisingly this came near to bankrupting the city: 'forasmuch as this city hath so long provided for the maintenance of the soldiers here for the defence thereof, that the treasure of this city is so farre exhausted'.[36] It was also necessary to increase food stocks to provide for around 1,500 extra mouths. In January 1643 the Common Council decreed

> For the provision of victuals in this City, it is thought fit and ordered that every inhabitant that contributeth to the relief of the poor shall

within the fourteen days next ensuing provide soe many bushells of pease as he or she is rated to pay weekly pence for the poor, uppon paine of 20 shillings apiece.

Corn was added to this in April.[37] Meanwhile, on 3 March 1643 a Committee was appointed to buy cattle.

Much of the administration of the defence remained with the Corporation. There was inevitably some overlap with the military commanders and Massey undoubtedly felt frustrated with the local politicians, exacerbated by the knowledge that he had not been their first choice as Governor, for they had initially wanted a local man. 'They thought well of a man neare home, and cast their eye on a knowne patriot. Nevertheless more intelligent men upon the serious review of the citie's continuall hazard, found that the necessity of this place did require a tried souldier.'[38] If this local 'knowne patriot' was Thomas Pury, later to be chairman of the Committee for the Defence of Gloucester, it might partly explain the antagonism that built up between them (see Appendix 1). The evidence of Massey's cut and thrust military campaigns do not suggest a man who would take any sort of bureaucratic interference lightly. Corbet agrees that 'the martial command was not fully settled.'[39] Massey could not choose captains of the Trained Bands and the Common Council also claimed the right of choosing the officers of the new City regiment formed in April 1643 which Massey later commanded himself (with Thomas Pury the elder and younger as two of the captains).[40]

MORALE

they were at their wits end, and stood like men amazed, feare bereft them of understanding and memory

So Corbet described the panic in Gloucester on the fall of Cirencester to Prince Rupert's army in 1643.[41]

The prospect of a siege was a terrifying one in seventeenth-century warfare. It would not have been an easy decision for the city to resist the King's direct appeal to surrender. At best they would face the prospects of a long drawn-out siege as the attackers tried to starve them out, with attendant risks of disease and the discomfort. At worst, under the conventions of the time if they refused to surrender then their town could be ruthlessly plundered. Before the Royalists took Marlborough in 1642 the commander announced 'if they compelled him to make his way and enter the town by force, it would not be in his power to keep his soldiers from that which they should win with their blood'.[42] What this could mean was graphically demonstrated when the Royalists took Exeter in September 1643 and they 'used the people most cruelly, and did all the violence they could to them'.[43] Prince Rupert had a particularly bad reputation in this respect. Later in the war, even the Royalist Clarendon seemed dismayed by his troops after Leicester fell in 1645. There the soldiers acted with 'the usual license of rapine and plunder, and miserably sacked the whole town, without any distinction of persons or places — churches and hospitals, as well as other houses, being made a prey to the enraged and greedy soldier'.[44]

Even if a town did agree terms after the siege had begun, the garrison, at least, could not be assured of fair treatment — as those ridiculed troops from Bristol found to their cost. Those recent events would not have been far from the minds of the citizens of Gloucester on 10 August. This fear extended to the Royalist sympathizers who had property within the city. A number sent a petition to the King begging him

> to give command to your commanders, and they to their severall officers and souldiers, that upon entrance to the city they forbeare to plunder any house until the loyall therein be distinguished from the disloyal.[45]

The resolve of the city had already been put under strain and Royalist sympathizers and worried neutrals were leaving the city. In April, Captain Husband deserted, leaving the city to worry about how to continue to supply his company.[46] The Corporation passed an act which disenfranchised burgesses and freemen who left the city for more than six days while the Earl of Stamford's Regiment was billeted in the city. The usual fine for re-admittance was £20.[47] There were eleven recorded instances of disenfranchisement but this, of course, only affected the wealthiest in the town. Sir Edward Walker, the King's Secretary of State, had compiled a list of 104 citizens in Gloucester that were deemed loyal to the king; it included notable citizens but was out of date for a number had clearly already been identified and arrested or had otherwise left the city.[48] One of those imprisoned was the pluralist, Dr John English, rector of Rudford, a

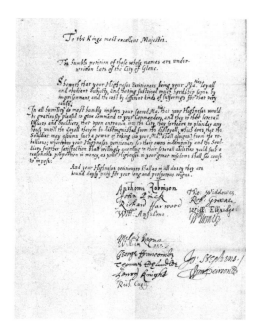

In anticipation of a Royalist victory at the siege, gentry appeal to King Charles to spare property in the town if it can be shown to belong to Royalist sympathizers. (*British Library, Harley MSS, 1608, f.114, with permission*)

prebendary of Gloucester Cathedral and curate of Cheltenham parish church. His memorial in Cheltenham church blames the death of his wife on this imprisonment. It reads:

> The sad memorial of John English, Dr in divinitie, to Jane, his most deare wife, . . . from whom he was divorced by eighteen months close imprisonment which soon after caused her death, on August 8th, 1643

Thomas Price was also on the list and later became sheriff (1661) and then mayor (1666), but he was already serving as a major in the King's Horse. Others included Mr Bell of Sandhurst who was one of the two 'pettifogging lawyers' that brought a personal appeal for the city to surrender on 24 August (he was later able to successfully claim duress on the grounds that his house was occupied by Royalist officers at the time).

The strength of such possible disaffection was taken very seriously, although it may also have been exaggerated to encourage further support from Parliament (Massey wanted an additional regiment) – or even to excuse an early surrender. On 29 July 1643 the City Council and Massey warned the House of Commons that the state of Gloucester was 'very ill'.[49] In a separate letter of the same day, Massey warned that the garrison – both officers and men – were so distrustful due to their lack of pay that he doubted their ability to fight. He went on to say

> Our wants are so great, and this city so averse to us, that our power cannot enforce men beyond their wills, which I had done, and would do so, if our regiment might have equalled the city in strength; but now, what with the general discontent of both, of the city soldiers and our own, we stand at present as betrayed unless speedily your care can prevent it . . . Alderman Pury and some few of the citizens, I dare say, are still cordial to us, but I fear ten for one incline the other way.[50]

This ratio of 10:1 against the prospect of action does not hold very well with the later expressions of unity during the siege. If there had been widespread grumblings then it was probably Thomas Pury, who had returned from London on the news of the surrender of Bristol, who deserves a large part of the credit in holding the city to its resolve. In a show of bravado the Corporation offered 'Whosoever was weak and faint-hearted, had leave to depart the city'.[51] Indeed, more people did leave after Royalist gentry in the county called upon the city to surrender on 2 August.[52] In a bid to try to ensure the loyalty of the garrison, there was a concerted effort to pay the men of at least the Town regiment (including Massey himself) immediately before the siege.[53]

Apart from the quite natural fear of being besieged and perhaps slaughtered, at the heart of the citizens' fears was the reluctance to be seen to be fighting against their king in person. This affected everyone from Massey downwards, although in the end it did not affect their actions. When the defenders on duty at one of the turnpikes on the approach road to the city first met the advancing Royalists they seem to have chatted amiably and the citizens declared 'if they knew the King were in the field, though their officers made them shoot, they would drop their bullets and vowed to drink the King's health on their knees'.[54] In an attempt to justify the failure of such men to follow through their words, *Mercurius Aulicus* reported on 24 August that the city 'filled the poor soldiers full of strong drinke, as the only meanes to make them stand'.[55] Massey may himself have been in contact with the King about a possible surrender. According to Clarendon he privately told a Royalist messenger from Col. Legge, his old commander from his time in the Scottish wars, that

> if the king himself came with his army, and summoned it [the city], he would not hold it against him, for it would not stand with his conscience to fight against the person of the king – besides that in such a case he should be able to persuade those of the town, which otherwise he could not do.[56]

This story was never confirmed elsewhere but according to Clarendon it was this message that tipped the scale in convincing the King to begin the siege – expecting a quick victory from a reluctant enemy.

In the event, loyalty to Parliament proved stronger. The disaffected received little support from anyone of influence; the lists of councillors during the Civil War period show a high degree of continuity as the leaders of the community stood united. During the siege the only recorded case of desertion was when 'that rogue Hatton, one of our canoneers, ran away to the enemy' on 20 August.[57] Clarendon admired how 'there was no one officer run from the town to him [the King], nor above three common soldiers, which is a great argument, the discipline within was very good'.[58] As another example of how the London press tried to maintain tension, an unconfirmed, and almost certainly false, report circulated in a parliamentary newspaper that before 29 August the mace-bearer and three to four other 'malignants' hid in a church steeple and intended to shoot Massey and other officers. A shot was claimed to have narrowly missed Captain Gray and the offenders were said to have been arrested, with the ring-leader hanged and the mace-bearer's fingers cut off.[59] This was not reported locally. Corbet stresses the unity within the city during the siege – overcoming past doubts and complaints as

> No great complainings were heard in our streets, no discontents seized on the souldiers, at other times prone to mutiny; men of suspected fidelity did not faile in action; every valuable person was active in his own place.

Chauvinistically, he admits surprise that even the women of the city played their part as 'the usuall outcryes of women were not then heard, the

'. . . the women of the City,
during the siege were so hardy as
to beare arms'. Women at War

weakness of whose sex was not overcome by the terrible engines of
warre'.[60] Indeed, the women may well have played a more active role than
even Corbet allows. The newsbook *Certain Informations from severall parts of
the kingdom* reported

> That the women of the City, during the siege were so hardy as to
> beare armes, and had a captain, and kept the watch in their turns,
> and when the Enemy had made a breach in the works, the women
> couragiously and fearlesly made it up, when the men durst not do
> it.[61]

Some further confirmation of this involvement comes from a letter in
the Blayney accounts in which Richard Phillips asks for a 'poor woman' to
be paid for bringing 'her team' (presumably a plough team) to the cathedral college – otherwise 'she will scratch my eyes out'.[62]

One reason for the unanimity of purpose is that, once the siege was
under way, Massey made it clear that surrender was a dangerous option –

'our late yeelding could not mollifie the King's army' and if the city did actually fall, then the defenders' best hope was to have impressed the attackers by their 'utmost gallantry' to win the best terms. His assessment was supported by the Royalists who threatened to hang the twelve alder-men from the signposts of the twelve inns in the town and also issued a more general threat of refusing quarter if the city had to be taken by force. On 3 September they shot a message into the city.

> These are to let you understand your god Waller hath forsaken you, and hath retired himselfe to the Tower of London. Essex is beaten like a dog; yeelde to the Kings mercie in time, otherwise, if we enter perforce, no quarter, for such obstinate traiterly rogues. From a well wisher.

The city replied in verse.

> Waller's no god of ours, base rogues, ye lie,
> Our God survives from all eternity;
> Though essex beaten be, as you doe say,
> Rome's yoke we are resolv'd nere to obey:
> But for our cabages which ye have eaten
> Be sure ere long ye shall be soundly beaten.
> Quarter we ask you none; if we fall downe,
> King CHARLES will lose true subjects with the
>   towne.[63]

Massey's arguments clearly worked – when relieved, the city had fought down to its last three barrels of gunpowder!

CHAPTER 4

The Siege of 1643: Defences

Bristol taking,
Exeter shaking,
Gloucester quaking

ROYALIST RHYME[1]

THE FORCES GATHER

The start of the siege was by way of a gradual build-up as the Royalists set up camps in the surrounding district to seal off the city from supplies and reinforcements. The Royalists set up their first camp on Tredworth Field (now the Park Road/Midland Road area to the east of the city) on Sunday 6 August. Captain Blunt from the city garrison led a scouting party to Wotton where they took ten prisoners before going on to Painswick where they spotted the assembling Royalist cavalry. The Royalists plundered Tuffley, 3 miles (4.8 km) south of the city, on 7 August and set up a base in 'Mr Wood's house' at Brookthorpe, 4 miles (6.4 km) to the south-east, where there was a skirmish. By Thursday 10 August; as well as a camp of six thousand foot and horse on Tredworth Field, the Royalist armies were now camped all around the city: to the south at Llanthony Priory; to the north at Walham (where two thousand cavalry were encamped), Kingsholm, Longford and London Road; Sir Jacob Astley was to the east at Barton; and Sir William Vavasour's Welsh army of up to four thousand men was on the west side of the Severn at Over. Cavalry were also quartered 7 miles (11.2 km) away at Newent. King Charles I himself arrived on 10 August and was quartered first at Painswick and then at Matson House (now Selwyn School), 2 $\frac{1}{2}$ miles (4 km) to the south-west of

Brookthorpe church. There was a skirmish around here and the orchard at the start of the 1643 siege, on 7 August

Gloucester, at the foot of Robinswood Hill. The ammunition magazine was close by, in Matson church. Prince Rupert based himself at Prinknash Park. Troops had been brought from Bristol, Worcester, Oxford and Wales. Lord Herbert (former commander of the Welsh forces) also provided 4,920 troops raised privately, despite having recently lost £60,000 as being the cost of his men and equipment captured at Highnam. He bitterly claimed after the war (1666–7) that

> at 14 dayes warninge I brought 4000 foote and 800 horse to the sidge of Glocester, payinge them £6000 down upon the naile at Glocester, besides my troope of Life Guards, consisting of six score noblemen and gentlemen, whose estates amounted to above three score thousand pounds a yeare, most of whom I furnished with horse and armes, which of a sudden they could not doe themselves . . .[2]

45

Local gentry had also been summoned to bring what forces they could raise to the siege. Lord Chandos's troop of horse included John Edwards of Shurdington armed with his 'sword, poleaxe and pistols'. Other named locals included Richard Bridges, clerk of Cromhall, who was accused later as being 'the activist man at the siege of Gloucester'. George Turbeville of Whitenhurst was a quartermaster to the army, and William Try of Hardwicke was in the King's Lifeguards. Nevertheless, some of the gentry chose to ignore the summons – including Sir John Wyntour who was to be so active after the siege. Estimates vary, but the total strength may have been as high as 30,000. One of the most urgent problems was how to supply this massive force. Charles I issued a proclamation from his Court at Painswick on 10 August that markets were to be set up in the camp where soldiers could buy food at 'reasonable' prices. The penalty for molesting or robbing anyone bringing food to the market was death 'without mercy'.[3] Command was to be in the hands of Patrick Ruthven, Earl of Brentford, who had been summoned from Oxford along with his siege train. He set up his headquarters at Llanthony. Prince Rupert had declined the overall command after his advice to storm the city had been

'Royalist camp' at the siege of Gloucester. (*M. Atkin with thanks to the 'Roundhead Association' of the ECWS and English Heritage*)

rejected but instead had an independent command of the cavalry.[4] The artillery was apparently under the command of young Henry, Lord Spencer.[5]

Against this the city could raise only between fourteen and fifteen hundred men (though probably augmented by other local irregulars). They also had around fifteen cannon. Some troops had actually been removed from the garrison, including two companies of Merrick's regiment who had probably met their fate with Waller at Roundway Down on 13 July. At the start of the siege they only had forty barrels of gunpowder but were then able to produce three barrels a week from two local powder mills. Lead had been stripped from 'The Vineyard' at Over to make musket balls in local foundries. The city had captured weapons from the Welsh at Highnam and also bought muskets, including the relatively new firelocks (flintlocks) and 'firepikes' (leather jacks fastened to the end of long pikes and filled with a burning, spitting material to deter the charging enemy during any possible street fighting). There was even a 'great crossbow' and a number of wooden clubs (see Appendix 3). The forces were an amalgam of parts of the Earl of Stamford's regiment, the Town regiment of about five hundred men raised in April 1643 and now commanded by Massey, together with the militia, officers and men of other broken units that probably became the nucleus of Col. (then Captain) Devereux's regiment from September, and a hundred men of a regiment of dragoons escaped from Bristol under Col. Forbes.[6]

Heralds were sent to the city at 2 p.m. on 10 August to read out Charles's proclamation for the city to surrender. The appeal was couched in conciliatory terms 'Out of our tender compassion to the City of Gloucester' with the promise of a free pardon if the city surrendered immediately. But, it also contained the warning to accept all responsibilities 'for all the calamities and miseries' that would befall if this offer was refused and Gloucester had to be taken by assault. It is probable that the King was expecting his terms to be accepted. However, after an interval of four hours (during which time the city made its last preparations for war), local bookseller, councillor and future mayor, Toby Jordan, and Sergeant Major Pudsey with 'lean, pale, sharp, and bad visages' (according to Clarendon) – representing civilian and military government in the city – brought the defiant reply which set the siege in motion.

We the inhabitants, magistrates, officers and souldiers within this garrison of Gloucester, unto his Majestie's gracious message returne

47

Matson House. Charles I commandeered Matson House (now Selwyn School) to use as his headquarters during the siege. The house itself was built around 1575. The King's quarters were in the first-floor range of the east wing, behind the sundial. The small quatrefoil window provides light to the privy

this humble answer, – That we doe keepe this city according to our oathes and allegiance to and for the use of his Majesty and his royall posterity, and doe accordingly conceive ourselves wholy bound to obey the commands of his Majesty, signified by both Houses of Parliament, and are resolved by God's helpe to keepe this city accordingly.[7]

They still claimed that they remained loyal to the King and would obey his orders – but only as presented through Parliament. But this was now a matter of mere convention. The die was cast and as the messengers returned 'Their backs turned scarce thirty yards, on clap they their caps in the King's presence, with orange ribbons in them'[8] – the orange ribbons being the general badge of the parliamentary side.

48

Matson House. Nicks in the window sill of one of the second-floor rooms of the east wing, looking towards Robinswood Hill. James II who, as a young prince (then nine years old) stayed at Matson House with his brother the Prince of Wales (then thirteen years old), later told Major-General William Selwyn: 'My brother and I were generally shut up in a chamber on the second floor at Matson during the day, where you will find that we have left the marks of our confinement inscribed with our knives on the ledges of the windows'

THE DEFENCES

The watching Royalists took this act of defiance as mere bravado. How could the city hope to resist such overwhelming odds? Although Gloucester had been feverishly working on its defences for over a year they were still unfinished at the start of the siege. The statement attributed to Waller in a parliamentary newsbook at the end of July that 'he found the Towne and Garison very strong and in a farre better condition than at first he imagined' can be put down to partisan journalistic enthusiasm.[9] In his letter of 29 July to Parliament, Massey had himself given an estimate that the city could only expect to hold out for six days without reinforcements of at least another regiment.[10] Much had to be done to remedy the defects in the defences during the siege itself.

By August 1643 and the start of the siege Corbet described the defences thus:

> The works of a large compass, not halfe perfect; from the south gate eastwards almost to the north port, the city was defended with an ancient wall lined with earth to a reasonable height; thence to the north-gate, with a slender work upon a low ground, having the advantage of a stone barn that commanded several wayes: [Whitefriars Barn] upon the lower part of the city, from the north to the west-gate, (being a large tract of ground) there was no ancient defence , but a small work newly raysed, with the advantage of mar- ish grounds without, and a line drawn within from the inner north- gate under the colledge wall to the priory of St Oswald's. From the west towards the south-gate along the river side, no more defence than the river itselfe, and the meadows beyond levell with the town: from the castle to the south-port, a firm and lofty work to command the high ground in the suburbs. The ditches narrow, but watered round.[11]

The Westgate bridges were also broken down according to Clarendon.[12]

The evidence suggests a number of distinct elements to the plan:

1) refurbishment of the medieval wall and ditch
2) newly-built bastioned lines
3) internal retrenchments
4) outworks
5) scorched earth policy in the suburbs.

1) Refurbishment of medieval defences

The medieval defences, consisting of a 2 m wide stone wall, 'two-stories high' and with a 4–5 m wide ditch in front, survived on the line to be enclosed in the Civil War only from the South Gate to the Almesham Postern at the north-east corner of the town (with a further surviving stretch to the Inner North Gate lying now within the circuit as an inner defence). A watching brief on 31 Parliament Street in 1984 revealed the

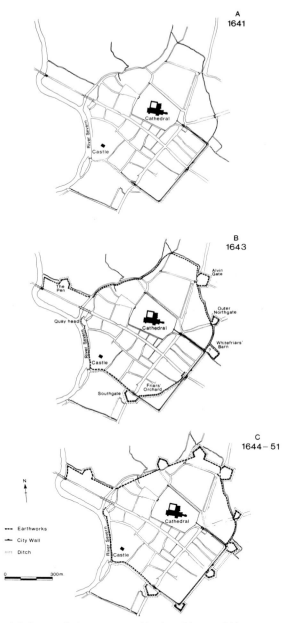

Post-medieval defences of Gloucester a) 1641; b) 1643; c) 1644–51

post-medieval or later backfills of the south ditch.[13] These defences had been designed for warfare from a bygone age and an obvious concern was to modernize them against the new threat of artillery barrage. The back of the wall was, therefore, lined with an approximately 1.5 m thick bank of earth to deaden cannon shot and to strengthen the wall generally. Some of the gate towers were also filled with earth. Further protection was provided for musketeers on top of the wall by the provision of wooden shields or 'blinds', and the ditches were cleaned out.

Despite there having been around twenty excavations on the line of the medieval defences, only a small number have shown possible evidence for the Civil War bombardment as the upper levels of the walls were razed in 1662. The upper courses of the section of wall excavated on Parliament Street in 1961 were displaced, suggesting that this might have been as a result of artillery fire.[14] In 1974, excavation on the south tower of the East Gate site revealed other possible evidence of bombardment in the form of

The south tower of the medieval East Gate under excavation in 1974 looking towards town. The East Gate was one of the principal targets of the Royalist artillery batteries. But evidence of this was confined to a large cannon ball which was found at the foot of the wall during the excavations. (*Gloucester City Museums*)

a spread of building rubble and debris, including a cannon ball, from outside the tower. The cannon ball weighed 6,940 grams (15 lb) and was of a
type fired from a culverin with a maximum range of 1,400 m (1,500
yards).[15] In addition, it is possible that alterations to the south-east corner
tower (in Friar's Orchard) may reflect Civil War strengthening, and that a
rebuild at the foot of the Roman wall along Brunswick Road may represent the repair of a breach.[16] Today the only surviving element of Civil
War activity on the defences is a small door or 'sally port' (now blocked) in
the south tower of the East Gate where six men were 'put forth at a port
hole in the dungeon at the East gate to intercept Royalist miners'[17]
(see p. 101).

2) Bastioned lines

The defences were to be much more than the simple patching up of the
existing fortifications. Much of the defences on the north side of the city
and additional defences around the gates had to be newly built as earthworks.

The first half of the seventeenth century saw considerable advances in
the techniques of urban defence, and many of the military engineers of the
English Civil War had gained their experience during the long and bitter
continental wars. The Dutch were considered to be the leaders in the field
through their experience during the 80-year war with Spain, and Col.
Massey had himself served with them as an engineer. The main characteristic of Dutch defences at the time was the earthen rampart behind a massive wet ditch. In its ideal form, the rampart would be unrevetted and
about 25 ft (7.6 m) high, with its base protected by a low outer rampart
(the *fausse-braye*) on the inner face of the ditch. It would be further protected by 'storm poles' projecting either from the side of the rampart or set
within the ditch to hinder advancing troops. The ditch was supposed to be
50 yards (46 m) wide and relatively shallow but with a deeper ditch, 6 m
wide, running down the centre. On the outer side of the ditch was a path-
way or 'covered way', protected by a sloping outer rampart (*glacis*). At
intervals along the defensive line were four-sided, and 'v'-fronted, angle
bastions. The design was intended to provide an uncomplicated and uni-
fied scheme of defence that kept attackers as far away as possible from the
principal line of defence and maximized the 'killing zone' if they attempted to attack. The bastions were sited so that they could rake the whole of
the open ground between them with 'enfilading' crossfire using musketry

Surveying early seventeenth-century town fortifications. From *Les Travaux de Mars*. (*Andrew Saunders, with thanks*)

and small artillery (rampart guns), and also to provide additional protection in front of gates.[18]

The Dutch defences were permanent features of towns at a time when constant war had become a normal fact of life. The defences of Gloucester were more hurried and therefore only show elements of the principle, concentrating on reinforcing the defences at the gates. Full use was made of natural features within the limited time available. The 'slender work' running from the Almesham Postern to the Outer North Gate was probably formed on the basis of the stream called the *King's Ditch*. The latter then joined the outer leg of the River Twyver or *King's Water* which ran towards the Alvin Gate. The course of the River Twyver here was recorded as an undefined feature during a watching brief on the construction of Black Dog Way in 1983.[19] If this hypothesis is correct then material for the attendant rampart must have been imported from elsewhere (see p. 71).

No sections have yet been excavated across the line of seventeenth-century modifications to the circuit ditch but these were probably similar

54

to their medieval antecedents. The line of the ditch also included a number of newly-constructed bastions on the Dutch pattern to provide additional protection around the gates. However, those actually completed by the time of the siege were too far apart to provide the principal aim of an effective crossfire along the whole length of the defences. Documented examples of bastions in 1643 were opposite St Oswald's Priory and at Little Meadow, as well as at the South, North and Alvin Gates. Dorney refers to cannon being mounted in 'the pen upon the west gate' and used against the Royalist cavalry based at Walham.[20] The Hall and Pinnell map also shows a bastion adjacent to Little Meadow, which was called 'Little Pen' on the Causton map of 1843. Dorney recounts how, on Friday 18 August, the Royalists mounted artillery 'against the Awneyate [Alvin Gate], and the sconces thereunto adjoining'.[21] Note that this account uses the term 'sconce' for what is described more precisely as a 'bastion' – the term 'sconce' being more properly reserved for a detached earthwork. It also talks in the plural, perhaps referring to separate artillery positions on each side of the bastion.

The Hall and Pinnell map of 1780 shows a more complex system of

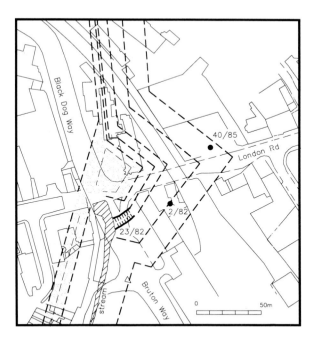

Plan of the 1643 bastion outside the Outer North Gate based on the evidence of a watching brief and the line of the unfinished outer ditch shown on the Hall and Pinnell map

bastions around the whole circuit, more in keeping with the Dutch ideal, but the context of this plan will be discussed later (p. 127). Here it will suffice to point out that Corbet specifically states that the Royalists in 1643 chose the east and south-east sides because the walls there lacked flankers and so they could 'make battery within pistoll shot of the walls'. New defences were hurriedly constructed behind the East Gate during the siege because 'the enemy having planted a store of canon baskets within half musketshot of the east gate point blank, intending a battery there'.[22] A bastion outside the East Gate itself would also have negated the siting of troops within the south tower to guard against mining.[23]

The first archaeological evidence of what is now interpreted as being a 1643 bastion came in a watching brief of 1982 on Bruton Way. A ditch at least 2.5 m deep and 8 m wide was found running diagonally between the London Road and George Street frontages, on the line of the east side of the bastion ditch as shown on the Hall and Pinnell map outside the Outer North Gate. A spur appears to have linked this ditch to the channel of the

View of the lower levels of the Civil War ditch excavated on the Southgate Gallery site in 1983. Note that the upper levels of the ditch had been destroyed by later foundations. Scale in half metres. (*Western Archaeological Trust*)

River Twyver running beside it and probably accounts for its asymmetrical plan.[24]

At the time there was no supporting evidence, other than the unlikely plan of Hall and Pinnell, to interpret the feature as being part of the Civil War defences.[25] Excavations outside the South Gate in 1983 and 1988/9 have now provided clear parallels; they confirmed the presence of a substantial, chevron-shaped defensive ditch on the line of the outer defence shown on the Hall and Pinnell map at that point.[26] A truncated profile of the bottom part of the ditch was revealed beneath a basement in 1983, with its true depth seen in the excavation of its outer lip in 1989. The full profile of the ditch proved to be 10 m wide and 4 m deep, steep-sided and cut through natural lias clay so that its bottom flowed with water. On the inner side of the ditch would have been the earthen rampart to provide shelter for the defenders. There was no surviving evidence of any sophisticated *fausse-braye* (which seems very unlikely, cf. the contemporary section drawn of the Newark fortifications), although evidence was found for a 30 m wide clearance on the outer side that would at least provide a clear 'killing zone' (any evidence for a glacis being destroyed). On the west side of the street was a medieval cellared building; its internally-buttressed walls

View of the 4 m deep Civil War ditch excavated on the Bank of England site, Southgate Street, during 1989. Note the steep, smooth sides cut through solid clay – easy to slide into but difficult to get out of! Scale in half metres. (M. *Atkin for Gloucester City Museums*)

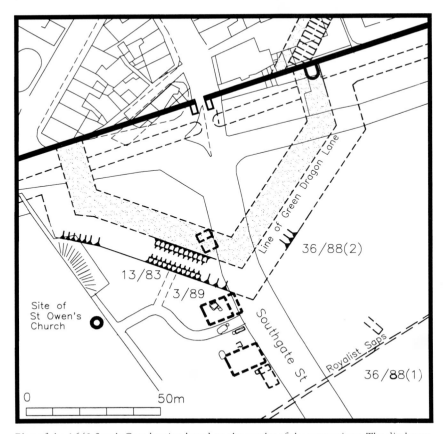

Plan of the 1643 South Gate bastion based on the results of the excavations. The ditch was 10 m wide and 4 m deep. No evidence was found for the rampart but one medieval building may have been incorporated within it as a blockhouse. The sites of the medieval houses lying immediately outside the defences had been levelled prior to the siege so as to provide a clear field of fire. Beyond these were found evidence of the Royalist trenches. The whole area had been levelled after the Civil War and the ground landscaped

survived the siege and may have been incorporated into the rampart as a blockhouse. It lay beside what has been interpreted as a drawbridge which, prior to the siege and afterwards, diverted the main approach to the South Gate across the line of the new defences. The evidence consisted of fragments of masonry embedded into the west side of the ditch and a localized restriction in the ditch's width.

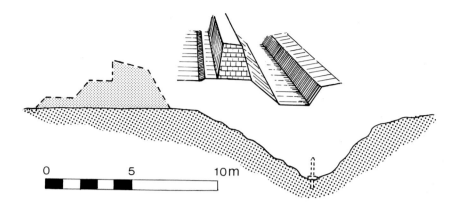

Contemporary section of redoubt earthworks from Newark (after Clampe's plan in Ashmolean Museum, Oxford), with profile of excavated Southgate Street bastion ditch for comparison

3) Internal retrenchments

Other defences were added actually during the siege as the Royalist plan unfolded. An inner line of above-ground defence to the South Gate was constructed on 13 August when the defenders

> began the blocking of the south port, making a damme of earth against the drawbridge, and a breast-work canon proofe against the wall reaching from the draw bridge to the gate, and lining the houses on each side, and the almes-house between the gate and the draw-bridge with earth.[27]

No evidence of this has yet been found.

On the south-west side of the city a 'half moon' shaped bastion was built on the 'Head of the Quay' – at the north end of modern Quayside, with a breastwork under the castle. This was to counter batteries built on Severn Street and Llanthony Road alongside the river and also to cover the approach from Westgate Bridge and 'The Island' if the main defences were breached on that side.

The siege was mainly directed at bombarding the area from the East to South Gates where the land was highest and driest, concentrating on the south-east corner where they could direct fire from two sides. They began

'We made a very strong work cross the street with a large trench before it . . .'. At the start of September the citizens feared that the defences at the East Gate were going to be broken and so started to dig an inner defence, blocking the line of Eastgate Street itself

to batter the south-east corner on 13 August and managed to create a breach on 14 August. The defenders quickly repaired this with wool sacks and gabions (large wicker baskets filled with earth or stones), but as the Royalists brought up faggots to try to fill the ditch on 17 August it was clear that a new assault could be expected. There was, indeed, a furious bombardment on 18 August against 'the corner of the wall next Rignall stile, making above one hundred and fifty great shot thereupon, where- with they shrewdly battered the wall, but our earthworkes stood firme'.[28] In expectation that the defences might eventually yield, an internal breast- work was dug between the East and South Gates across the open ground of Friar's Orchard on 19 August 'so making up all passages into the town betweene that and the east-gate', with a 'sconce' constructed in Friar's Orchard from 1 September.[29] A number of houses appear to have been razed in front of this to prevent them being used as cover: 'the houses were fired round aboutt neare the gates'.[30] The sconce was designed to carry four

Cheveaux de frise or wooden 'storm poles' that were set in the bottom or sides of the Civil War ditch to impede an enemy. This example was recovered while recording a sewer tunnel, from the bottom of the 1644–51 bastion ditch on the south-east angle of the defences. (*P. Greatorex for Gloucester City Museums*)

cannon and to be able to cover the area within the walls and also the east flank if the defences at the East Gate gave way.

The East Gate came to be seen as the weakest point of the defences. Additional defences were constructed across Eastgate Street itself on 3/4 September, after the Royalists had renewed mining operations, and were to form a secondary line of defence if the Royalists broke through the gate. Dorney describes how 'We made a very strong work crosse the street [Eastgate Street] with a large trench before it, and filled it with water, intending to raise it up to the eaves of the houses, and to plant some cannon there'.[31] This may be equated with an irregularly-profiled 7 m wide and 3 m deep ditch cutting across Eastgate Street and lying 20 m behind the gate itself, as seen in a watching brief of a new sewer in 1990.[32]

In the event, the siege was lifted on 5 September before these, literally, 'last ditch' defences had to be tested. For the inhabitants they must have appeared as an ominous signal of impending doom.

4) Outworks

The city had also prepared a series of outer defences on the west and north-west (river) side which had helped to keep the Welsh army out of the city in March. In the event these had to be abandoned at the start of the siege on 10 August leaving defence to the flooding of the marshes.[33] Two sconces had been made at each end of Alney Island (a marshy area between the two arms of the River Severn) to secure the river.[34] The west channel of the River Severn was also protected by The Vineyard, Over (see p. 64) and possibly by a zig-zag trench, running between the two arms of the river, shown on the 1734 Buck prospect, and which was originally a ditch dividing Town Ham from Maisemore Ham. This was taken over by the attacking Royalists. On 2 September the Welsh from The Vineyard 'placing themselves in a ditch, they played upon our maides and workmen that were fetching turffes out of the little meade'.[35]

The Vineyard, Over, is the best surviving earthwork of the siege, with a plan similar to works such as the Queen's Sconce at Newark.[36] The former palace of the bishop of Gloucester was refortified in March 1643 to keep watch on the Royalist force at Highnam 1 1/2 miles (2.4 km) to the west. A new, shallow ditch incorporating artillery emplacements on the west-facing corners was added to the medieval moated site – the ditch of which may have been recut and enlarged to a scale comparable with that of the city ditch. Dorney, with malicious pleasure, describes the 'capture' of the

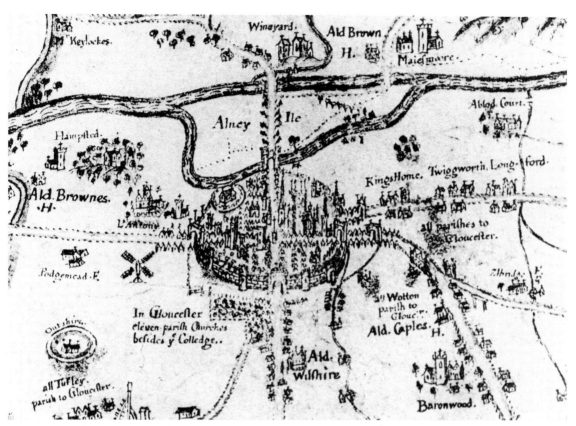

Map of Gloucester 1624, showing the Hundreds of Dudston and Kings Barton. Like the Speed map (p. 2), it shows the surviving medieval walls from the South Gate to North Gate. Note the reference to the Wineyard (Vineyard) and Wainlode Hill. The map also shows the extent of the suburbs – compact on the south side but more extensive along Barton Street, and with the then hamlets of Barnwood and Hucclecote along Ermin Street and Kingsholm, Twigworth and Longford to the east. In all, the authority of Gloucester at the time of the siege extended over 45 square miles (116.5 km). (*Gloucester Collection, Gloucester City Library, with permission*)

'The Welsh forces under Sir William Vavasor advanced to the Wineyard . . .'. Air view of the former Bishop's Palace ('the Vineyard') at Over, converted into a redoubt in 1643. (*Gloucester City Council*)

'. . . upon their entry of the outward worke . . .'. The shallow outer ditch of the Over earthwork is visible here as a band of thistles, with the remains of the inner bank to the left. The scale is in half metres

'. . . when they saw another within, they . . . immediately ran out'. The inner ditch of the Over earthwork is on a massive scale, comparable to that dug around the city itself. The scale is in half metres

site *after* it had actually been abandoned and burnt down by Col. Forbes's dragoons on 10 August (but not before they had stripped it of its lead to make musket balls).

> The Welsh forces under Sir William Vavasor advanced to the Wineyard, where after tow houres solemnity, they with great valour tooke it, no body being there to make a shot against them. Yet upon their entry of the outward worke, when they saw another within, they according to their knowne prowesse, immediately ran out, yet taking heart againe, they at last, to their eternall glory, tooke it.[37]

Despite the generally low opinion of the Welsh army of the time, Charles I expressed a naïve pleasure at his reception from them on a tour of his forces at the siege for he 'did rejoyce much at the Welshmen for they did throw their caps and hallow much with joye'.[38]

5) Scorched earth policy in the suburbs
The construction of the defences in 1642–3 involved considerable destruction before the period of the actual siege. Excavation on the Bank of

England site has shown that on the east side of Southgate Street a complete medieval street, Green Dragon Lane (cutting across the modern junction of Southgate Street and Parliament Street) was destroyed in digging the ditch.[39] The sunken way of the Lane provided a convenient alignment. As well as the line of the ditch, a corridor would have needed to be cleared on both sides for rampart, counterscarp bank, 'covered way' or simply an open 'killing zone'. Archaeological evidence of this clearance came from the west side of Southgate Street (Southgate Gallery site) where a 30 m wide corridor was cleared outside the ditch with the ground level in part stripped down by 0.5 m to the Roman surface.[40]

Two other streets and their adjacent houses were also destroyed immediately outside the defences. Fete (Fetter) Lane lay outside the Alvin Gate and Brook Street lay just outside the north-east corner (adjacent to the medieval Whitefriars). Brook Street was only partially rebuilt after the siege (now Station Road).[41] The City Chamberlain's Accounts describe how houses were 'digged up for the fortifications', 'Taken into the works' or 'Taken down by order'[42] while the Blayney Accounts for 5 August 1643 itemize 'Payd divers workmen for pulling down of houses by order of sergeant Major Ferrer'.[43] One medieval cellared building was excavated on Southgate Street in 1989 which lay 27 m from the point of the defences; it had been demolished around the time of the siege but there was no evidence of any burning on its walls or other debris in the cellar. It appears that this was one of those buildings 'digged up' and its cellar then backfilled so as not to provide any cover. One of the most notable casualties of this precautionary clearance was the tower of Llanthony Priory – demolished before June 1643 to prevent it being used for artillery spotting by any attacker.[44] If such action demanded careful planning and a strong resolve, worse was to come. Contingency plans had been drawn up by at least June 1643 for the demolition of the rest of the buildings within the suburb in the event of attack – 241 houses in all, one-third of the houses in Gloucester – so that they could not be used as cover by any besieging Royalist army. This must have created an organizational nightmare and on 20 June a committee was established to find housing for the inhabitants of the suburbs should it prove necessary to move them 'to consider whether such persons whose houses are to be pulled down in the suburbs may be conveniently placed in houses within the City'.[45] Unfortunately we have no surviving record of how this billeting was to be arranged.

The contingency plan was put into operation on the afternoon of 10 August when the citizens 'after the returne of our messengers, fired all our suburbs on the north, east and south parts, as being those that could and would have done us most harme'.[46] The fires were reported as being started in three places at once (presumably one in each suburb), and more houses were fired on the following night. The destruction affected rich and poor alike. It included the manor houses of Kingsholm and the house of Alderman Powell in South Ward – among the properties that Clarendon described as 'large and fair buildings' – but also large numbers of poorer-quality rented properties including fifty houses owned by Thomas Dennis in the South Ward. In all, the 241 houses were valued at £28,720 including contents valued at £4,000.[47] Individual values ranged from the £10 of Mrs Hayward's cottage to the £500 house of Mr Mitchell, both in North Ward. The Chamberlain's Accounts for 1644 contain a number of entries for non-payment of rent with the explanation in the margin 'burnt at the siege of 1643'.[48]

Item Mr James Powell for the Inne & Pasture ground called the White Lyon without the Southgate and for a garden adjoining for one yeare's rent (Inn burnt & ground layd wast 1643) 4-2-0d.[49]

'. . . in the shadow and shelter of houses which the flames had not catched'. Lenda Antiques, Southgate Street. This is the sole survivor of the razing on the south suburb on the afternoon of 10 August 1643. It lies just beyond the turnpike and was therefore probably occupied by the Royalists before the citizens could burn down the rest of the suburb

Yet this destruction was not total. During the siege it is reported how the Royalists began to dig their siegeworks in the south and east suburbs 'in the shadow and shelter of the houses which the flames had not catched'. Indeed, it appears that the Royalists may have burnt down some houses themselves.[50] One house in the east suburb survived because its surrounding gardens acted as a firebreak; a number of sixteenth-century cottages survived on Barton Street until 1984. In the Southgate suburb, the one surviving fifteenth-century building (now Lenda Antiques) lay just beyond the turnpike in the Littleworth district (approximately on the line of the present entrance into the Docks from Southgate Street), which marked the extent of the land that the Royalists held before the suburb was fired. One of the most oft-quoted casualties of the razing was the church of St Owen, which had stood on the west side of Southgate Street, outside the gate. Its destruction is described thus in an Ordinance of April 1648: 'St Owen's, pulled down and demolished immediately before the late siege of Gloucester'.[51] Parts of the church fittings were certainly used in the repair of St Mary de Crypt schoolroom on Southgate Street in 1648. The lead from the roof was stripped and some stone from the foundations was used in repaving the adjacent street. The Chamberlain's Accounts contain the entries: 'Received more of Mr Anthony Edwards of leadd remayning in his hands being City ledd weighing xxiiij cwt which was used upon the Southgate which came from St Owen's Church' [52] and 'Paid to Thomas Deane & James Laurence for fower daies work a peice in digging of stones out of St Owen's Church foundations at xijd per day 0-8-0d'.[53] The family of Dennis Wise had been buried in St Owen's churchyard and he, as 'the twentieth Child of his said father, and sole Survivor at this time of all the rest of his said Brethren and Sisters', repaired a monument in the Cathedral in memory of one at St Owen's described as 'being defac'd and ruinated by the dissolving and taking down of the Parish Church of St Ewens, without the South gate of this City, in the late unhappy Wars and Divisions of this Kingdom'.[54]

The site of the demolished church was finally destroyed during the construction of the Docks in 1847 but was pinpointed on the Southgate Gallery excavation in 1989 by the alignment of the two medieval lanes that ran towards it. But excavation has shown that its fate at the siege proved to be not so simple. The stone foundations of an eighteenth-century brick-walled parsonage built on the street frontage were almost

'. . . digged up for the fortifications'. Late fifteenth-century cellared building in the Southgate suburb, excavated on the Southgate Gallery site in 1989. There was no evidence for any burning within the cellar and it was probably one of those houses that was demolished well before the start of the siege in order to provide a clear field of fire. (*P. Greatorex for Gloucester City Museums*)

totally composed of stone robbed from the church and that fragments of chancel arch showed signs of having stood in an exposed state for some time. Other fragments still had evidence of eighteenth-century paintwork, suggesting that parts of the structure had been refurbished at that time. Physical evidence for the razing of the suburbs on 10 August remains slender. The buildings would burn very quickly, the fire passing from one roof to another. However, the stumps of the charred main timbers would still remain standing and other fragments of timbers may have been scattered around within mounds of ash around 15–20 cm thick. Unfortunately nothing like this has been found in an excavation in the city to date. The walls of one building partially excavated on the Bank of England site did show some evidence of burning and its floors were covered with thin layers of charcoal, but evidence was otherwise confined to only thin spreads of charcoal flecking blown across the area of the Southgate Street excavations.

The likelihood is that such remains of fire damage were cleared away during the landscaping of around 1648.

In the light of such destruction it is a measure of the commitment of the citizens that no complaints have survived by the inhabitants of the suburbs. This may be contrasted to the situation in Exeter in 1645 when such destruction was forced on the population by the then occupying Royalist army in advance of a siege by Parliament's 'New Model Army'. There the Royalist governor made

> fuell of the Inhabitants houses, converting whole streets into ashes, to make the Town (as he sayes) the more tenable, turning out the people to the mercy of the Besiegers, where they find more humanity from an enemy than their supposed friends.[55]

Equally to try to deny the Royalists an easy approach to the city, the citizens flooded the water meadows and low-lying land on the north and

'Burnt at the siege'. A number of the city accounts contain marginal notes to explain the non-payment of rents because the properties had been 'Burnt at the Siedge' or 'Taken into the Works'. (*Gloucestershire Records Office, with permission*)

north-west sides of the city.[56] This may explain the men employed on
defence work around Dockam Ditch in 1642–3 (see Appendix 3) as they
prepared sluices ready to flood the land if necessary.[57]

THE LABOUR OF DEFENCE

> All suspended private cares, and the women and children acted their
> parts in making up the defects of the fortifications. . . . It was
> admirable to observe . . . the cheerful readinesse of yong and old of
> both sexes, as well of the better as inferiour sort of people by day and
> night, to labour in the further fortification of our citie.[58]

Thus did Corbet describe the 'both expensive and tedious' defence work of
1642–3. Clearly the whole community – men, women and children – was
involved in this enterprise.

The ditches had to be cut by hand to a depth of up to 4 m and through
solid lias clay, with the earth piled up behind to form the rampart. On the
north side of the city, the defenders made use of the line of the River
Twyver and the marsh, and here the soil for the rampart would have had to
be carted in from further afield. Evidence of soil stripping in fields alongside the River Twyver in Kingsholm (in the area of the present rugby
ground, behind St Mark Street) may represent large-scale quarrying for the
city defences.[59] Much of the work in lining the city walls on the south and
east sides with earth was undertaken after the start of the siege (see p. 59)
when opportunities for quarrying would be limited. Thus it is also possible that rectangular features shown on the 1610 Speed map within 'The
Paddock' to the north of the Cathedral, and interpreted as fishponds, were
later extended into irregular quarry pits as shown on the Hall and Pinnell
map and recorded in a watching brief in 1989.[60] Other material may have
been quarried from adjacent to the former castle ditches and on 'Bareland'
in the west of the city. Excavation in 1991 on the site of the gardens
attached to Thomas Bell's mansion on Blackfriars Way/Ladybellegate
Street (formerly the Dominican Friary) suggested that the ground level
had certainly been stripped off here in the seventeenth century to a depth
of over 1.2 m – enough to expose the burials of the underlying Friary burial
ground – and this material may well have been used to line the adjacent
south defences.[61]

'Our maids and others wrought daily without the works in the little mead, in fetching in turfe in the very faces of our enemies.' Women and children cutting turf to build ramparts for the defences

Remarkably, some turf was still collected – by the women – from outside the defences in Little Meadow (now the Cattle Market area) on the north-west side of the city during the siege when 'Our maids and others wrought daily without the works in the little mead, in fetching in turfe in the very faces of our enemies'.[62] This partly explains a claim in the *Presentation of the Grand Jury to Parliament* in 1646 for 'The little mead and meanham and other grounds, being drown'd from the beginning of the wars, and so remaineth'.[63] The fact that animals were being grazed in these areas during the siege means that it was not simply that all of the area had been deliberately flooded (although some undoubtedly was). Other land was being progressively de-turfed and turned into a morass. It is possible that in this case the turf was collected to dry for fuel, rather than for use in the defences, as supplies of coal had been cut off. Turf was certainly collected as fuel in London during the Civil War.[64]

There is little direct information as to how this labour was organized during the actual siege period, although it is clear that the poor were put to work there.[65] Councillors made daily inspections to ensure that money raised by the Committee for Defence was being properly spent.[66] Some idea of possible arrangements comes from the surviving documentation of the post-siege defences. In 1644 the Quarter Sessions ordered that all tenants should work at the fortifications at the rate of one day's work for every yard of land (the width of their tenements).[67] On 25 August 1651

> all burgesses and inhabitants of Glocester, who are not listed, are to muster by themselves, servants or workmen tomorrow morning by six o'clock, with spades, shovels and mattocks and little baskets at the south gate, to work at the fortifications all that day upon pain of 5s a piece.[68]

MANNING THE DEFENCES

Arrangements for manning of the defences, at least before the siege itself, were under the organization of the Common Council. Duty on the watches by the citizens, including the Trained Bands, was not popular and new

The church of St Mary de Crypt, Southgate Street, was used as the main ammunition magazine during the siege. The schoolroom to its north was repaired in 1648 using material taken from the ruins of St Owen within the Southgate suburb

73

regulations to improve attendance by threatening imprisonment or fines were regularly made throughout the Civil War period.[69]

During the siege, the number of the garrison would only allow an average ration of one man per 2.3 m along the defended circuit if they were evenly distributed. The paucity of numbers would have been made worse by the frequent assignment of troops to raiding parties and sallies. The latter could involve up to four hundred men by report – nearly one-third of the garrison – which would have left the city extremely vulnerable at those times. So the forces were concentrated at the main strategic points on the circuit of the East, West, South, North and Alvin Gates, the Almesham Postern, Barbican Hill, the castle and the quay. Inside the city, reserves were posted at St Mary's, the Marshalsea, St Katherine's, the College, the Boothall, the Tolsey and Lower Tolsey to be assigned to the circuit as necessary. A main guard of 120 men was at the Wheat Market on Southgate Street near The Cross, with the men on permanent duty to act as a flying reserve in case of attack. An order of November 1642 detailed how 'those upon dead quarters [were] to assist where the greatest service is'.[70]

The main magazine was in St Mary de Crypt. This needed some repairs to make it suitable, as accounts detail the 8s 4d spent on making brick walls and repairing the roof.[71] There was a stock of only forty barrels of powder at the start of the siege but two powder mills (at the quay and in cathedral outbuildings) were able to replenish supplies (even so there were only three barrels left at the lifting of the siege). They were obviously working to their maximum capacity. Indeed, one broke down soon after the siege and had to be repaired. A number of payments were made immediately after the siege (9 September) for work in the powder mills during the siege itself. There was £9 6s 0d to Thomas David 'the powder maker' and £3 11 0d to Thomas Barnes for his fortnight's work in making the saltpetre (potassium nitrate – mixed with sulphur and powdered charcoal to make gunpowder). On 30 September £1 2s 6d was paid for hauling saltpetre liquor to the mill and 11s 5d for making tubs and barrels to put the powder in.[72]

CHAPTER 5

The Siege of 1643: Tactics

A city assaulted by man but saved by God ever remember the Fifth of September, 1643, give God the glory

THE ROYALISTS SURVEY THE SCENE

The three basic tactics to be employed in a siege were either to try to starve the population into submission – a process which might take months – or to take the town by military action either 'by approach' (by a careful build-up to an attack on a point of weakness) or 'by storm' (a direct frontal assault). From the start the Royalists seem to have had a confused approach as to what to do – indeed many thought that the whole idea was a mistake, if not a parliamentary plot! Henry, Lord Spencer, wrote of his own doubts to his wife Dorothy on 9 August (see Appendix 2, p. 171). During the siege the Queen was reported to be very angry that her advice had not been heeded 'that to speak of the loss the king's forces have received at Gloucester is as bad at Oxford as treason'.[1] *Mercurius Britanicus* spoke of the Queen being in tears at the waste of resources.[2] Clarendon added his view that the king had 'neither money nor materials requisite for a siege'.[3]

When they arrived before Gloucester the Royalists were expecting a quick surrender and may never have intended to mount a tight or prolonged siege, while the king was opposed to a storm assault as had recently been used at Bristol. The bloodshed at the latter had shocked Charles for whom civil war remained an anathema. 'It is a hard and disputable choice for a king that loves his people and desires their love either to kill his own subjects or be killed by them'.[4] The odds seemed easily on their side with an army of up to thirty thousand men facing a garrison of only around one thousand four hundred. Experienced Royalist officers, including Prince Rupert, Sir Arthur Aston, Sir Jacob Astley and Major Legge rode around the defences and concluded that they were in such a poor condition that they could be taken within ten days. They were described as 'but of an old stone wall, which would fall upon an early battery'. This assessment seems to have been supported by their opponents. The disgraced commander of fallen Bristol, Nathaniel Fiennes, later repeated the contention that contemporaries on the parliamentary side believed after the fall of Bristol 'that they would be hanged if Gloucester could hold out two days, if the enemy came before it'.[5] Massey had told Parliament that he believed he could hold out at most for six days without reinforcements.[6] According to Clarendon (perhaps repeating Walker's assessment) they also believed

> that there were many well-affected people in the town, who, with those who were incensed by the burning of the suburbs, and the great losses they must sustain thereby, would make such a party, that as soon as they were distressed, the seditious party would be forced to yeild.[7]

The recommended tactic was therefore by approach, 'for all thoughts of storming were laid aside upon the loss of [?at] Bristol'.[8]

SEALING THE CITY

Although an attempt was made to cut the water supply by blocking the conduits running from the springs on Robinswood Hill and diverting the River Twyver, there is no evidence for any outer line of circumvallation to securely blockade the city. In part, this was probably thought unnecessary due to the concentration of troops around the city and the belief that it would be impossible to raise a serious relief force to come to the city's aid. Vavasour's Welshmen were there to seal the area west of the Severn while the actual assault was planned from camps ringing the city on the other sides. Patrols were put out that were evidently effective as Corbet states 'The straitness of the siege debarred all intelligence'. This was not completely true as the city was able to put watchmen on Wainlode Hill to

Lady Well on Robinswood
Hill. This formed the head
of the medieval system of
piped water that served
the city. The water supply
was cut at the start of the
1643 siege

give a signal of any approaching relief army, and some messengers did
penetrate the Royalist lines to Warwick. But it is also clear that other
messengers did not get through and there is no evidence to suggest that
the city was in any way resupplied outside its own resources. This over-
confidence allowed some bizarre examples of laxity in the immediate confinement of the city; for example on 30 August, 'This day we turned out
our cattle to graze in the little meade, and so continued them afterwards,
guarded by some muskettiers, taking them in at night: we made a bridge
of ladders, and thereby put them in over the workes'. Over two hundred
cattle were so grazed.[9]

In the event, the siege was raised before it could have been expected to
bite in terms of starving the population out. Although ammunition was
getting dangerously low, food was apparently still plentiful and there are
no accounts of disease as beset Bristol during its second siege.

ATTRITION

The main tactic of the siege was a hesitant battle of attrition fought in the
trenches and from artillery positions, intended to build up to a final
assault through breaches caused by mines and sapping. This was not a
campaign of set-piece engagements but of a mix of long-range artillery

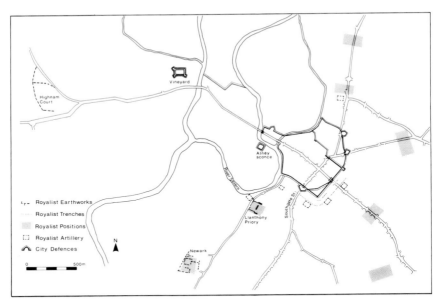

The Royalists established themseves in a number of separate camps and batteries but there was no outer line of 'circumvallation' to ensure a tightly-controlled siege

bombardment and intense hand-to-hand fighting with opposing positions less than a pistol range apart.

The main intent of the Royalist plan is clear from Appendix 1. Their first target was the south-east corner of Gloucester which was the high ground and once a breach was made here the attackers could expect to sweep down through the rest of the city. It was also easier to dig approach trenches and mines here than in the boggier ground to the west. At the start of the siege they began to build a battery in Gaudy Green (now off Brunswick Road) with three cannon of 5 lb, 14 lb and 22 lb and then one or more mortars, and started digging trenches towards the defences. On 16 August they were extending operations to the north side of the East Gate towards Friar's Barn (the north-east corner of the old medieval defences). Two days later they were installing cannon in Kingsholm, but any attempt to launch an assault from there was thwarted by a sally which spiked the cannon.[10]

If this was all part of an attempt to launch an attack over a broad front from the South Gate to Kingsholm, it was abandoned and the next move

Aerial view of Gloucester looking south-west. This shows the surviving line of the Roman south and east defences around the curve of Parliament Street and Brunswick Road. Much of the action of the siege of 1643 took place on this part of the defences. One of the main Royalist artillery batteries was on Gaudy Green which succeeded in making a breach in the city defences, although further attacks here were repulsed. The line of the bastion created outside the South Gate is also shown, based on the results of excavations 1983–9. St Mary de Crypt was the main ammunition store during the siege. (*Russell Adams, copyright Gloucester Newspapers Ltd, with thanks*)

was to redouble the assault on the south-east corner (building an additional battery of three guns), firing over one hundred and fifty shot there on 19 August. From 28 August there seems to have been a new emphasis on mining the East Gate. It is possible that the ultimate plan was for simultaneous breaches of the East Gate and the south-east corner in order to occupy the high ground in the city. The direction of the threat was appreciated by the city, who feverishly sought to repel the sapping towards the south-east corner and started to build additional internal defences to

View along Brunswick Road towards the curve of the south-east corner of the defences into Parliament Street. This clearly shows how the defences were designed to cover the high ground, with the present road dipping down along Brunswick Road further to the south. There was no bastion here during the siege itself, but one of the houses outside the defences is still called 'Bastion House' (left of view); archaeological evidence for a bastion believed to have been constructed 1644–51 was found during sewer workings in 1982/4 and 1990

prepare for the eventuality of losing that whole side of the city between the East and South Gates (see p. 59). It seems likely that the Royalists only began to seriously plan a direct assault on the city from 26 August, when they intensified work to fill the ditch by Rignall Stile and prepare mines under the East Gate. Fortunately for the city, their plans were interrupted in the early stages by the arrival of the Earl of Essex's relief column.

The Royalist plan of assault consisted of three main elements:

1) artillery bombardment
2) digging of assault trenches (saps)
3) mining.

These were supported by attempts to destroy the morale of the defenders.

1) Artillery

The artillery bombardment served a number of purposes. It was directed to concentrate fire on sections of the defences where an assault was planned, in the hope of pounding a hole through them. Cannon might also be loaded with 'grape shot' to use against troop concentrations, and evidence of a temporary field forge making the small iron balls for this was found in a field at Longlevens on the north-east side of the town. Artillery was also used to cause general damage within the town, by attempting to set the houses alight with red-hot shot (as fired from the Llanthony battery). The Civil War claims the distinction of being the first occasion in English warfare where artillery had been used against 'civilian' targets on a widespread scale in order to create both physical damage and terror. The King presumably brought the siege guns recently used to such good effect at Bristol and also summoned a siege train from Oxford. In all there were claimed to have been about one hundred and forty cannon at the siege. Forty miners from the Forest of Dean were impressed to repair the artillery train.[11]

The cannon were grouped in batteries within rectangular emplacements defended with 2 m high wicker cannon baskets ('gabions') filled with earth or stones, and also by ditched earthworks as documented by Dorney in the square redoubt at Gaudy Green. He described how 'At the first they cast uppe a dyke neare the South side of the gate, to plant their ordinance, & so they continued digging for many daies, and planted more ordinance

The now secluded close of Gaudy Green was the site of one of the main Royalist artillery batteries during the siege, aiming fire at the south-east corner of the city defences

Various types of ammunition. The large cannon ball (15 lb/8 kg) is from a culverin and
was found during the Eastgate excavations. The smaller (4 lb 10 oz/2.1 kg) is from a saker
and has been marked with the arrow of the King's ordinance. Part-finished iron grape shot
found at Longlevens. There may have been a temporary forge making ammunition here.
Lead musket balls of varying calibres. (*P. Greatorex for Gloucester City Museums*)

along fryers orchard, betwixt the Southgate and the Eastgate'.[12] No defin-
ite evidence of such a battery now survives but it may have consisted of a
low, raised platform incorporating an approximately 3 m high rampart to
the front and with a shallow ditch around it. A 2 m deep ditch found on
Cromwell Street (see p. 91) may have been associated with a battery at
Rignall Stile.

One eyewitness told Sergeant Foster that three to four hundred great
shot had been fired during the siege.[13] Gunnery was a dangerous occupation in the seventeenth century: the engineers in charge wore heavy siege
armour to protect themselves but were key targets. Two cannoneers at
Gloucester were killed during a sally and three others by sniper fire. Siege
weapons at the start of the Civil War tended not to be too effective as
there were not enough guns of the larger calibres needed for reducing
defences. At the siege of Gloucester, Royalist cannon ranging from 15 lb

to 25 lb are referred to, of the types from culverin to demi-cannon. The largest, the demi-cannon, was fired from the Llanthony battery, with a range of around 1,000 m. This type demanded a gun crew of three gunners and six assistants (matrosses), and was drawn by a team of five oxen or seventeen horses. It was later classed as being the minimum size required for a siege.[14] No mention is made of the larger, more specifically siege guns, such as the 46 lb cannon or 64 lb cannon royal.

Most terrifying of the weapons were the mortars that fired the 'grenadoes' as used from Gaudy Green. These were artillery pieces with a short barrel and very wide bores that fired with a high trajectory but low velocity, in order to drop an explosive shell down on to the target. These weapons were commonly set within rectangular pits or earthworks. The projectile was a hollow iron sphere ('grenado') filled with powder and a slow burning fuse that was designed to explode the shell into shrapnel just before, or as, it landed. They could also be used as incendiaries, firing a

'They began a most furious battery upon both sides of the corner of the wall neare the Rignall stile, making above 150 great shot thereupon . . .'. A Royalist artillery battery in action

mixture of sulphur and saltpetre wrapped in a pitched canvas cover.[15] It was reported to Sergeant Foster for his *Perfect Diurnal* that twenty grenadoes were fired in the siege, and shells of up to 60 lb were used (although shells of over 150 lb are known from elsewhere). There were so few because they were so expensive. Although terrifying and potentially devastating to the inhabitants of a besieged town, they appear to have caused surprisingly little damage here. Fortunately the 'grenadoes of great weight, which when they fell in the citie were red as fire; yet blessed be God, kild not one man therewith'.[16] The effectiveness of the mortars depended on the shell exploding at the right time and the gunners at Gloucester seem to have used fuses that were too long. The shells either buried themselves in the earth, putting themselves out as 'they tore up the ground as if a bear had been rooting up the earth' or gave sufficient time for the citizens to extinguish them. Dorney relates how 'one fell into the street near the South gate, but a woman coming by with a payle of water, threw the water thereon, and extinguished the phuse [fuse] thereof, so that it did not break'.[17]

One mortar shell 'fell into the street near the South gate, but a woman coming by with a payle of water, threw the water thereon, and extinguished the phuse [fuse] thereof, so that it did not break'

They did pose a fearsome danger to the gun crews themselves. On 12 August it is described how 'we have since received intelligence from some that were the whole leaguer in the King's army, that their biggest morter-piece brake at the first discharging of it; they say the biggest in England'.[18] This incident has been suggested as one alternative explanation for the origin of the Humpty Dumpty rhyme.

In return the city had about fifteen artillery pieces, the largest apparently being demi-culverins.[19] A sacre and drake are also specifically mentioned. The cost of the artillery was a major part of the expenses faced by the city council before the siege. A number of the accounts detail the costs of providing necessary parts including their carriages, wheels and soap to oil them, lead to make protective aprons beside the cannon, linstocks, powder horns, match and skins for sponges to clean out the barrels after firing (see Appendix 3).

One story exults in the accuracy of the city's gunners, firing at Llanthony from the barbican which lay between the angle of what is now Barbican Road and Commercial Road (a distance of 650 m). On Thursday 31 August:

Siege armour dating to around 1680. Similar armour may have been used by engineers at Gloucester in 1643. The armour was extra thick to maximize protection to those directing fire and surveying the trenches. Note especially the plates designed to carry the weight of the helmet on to the shoulders. (*The Board of Trustees of the Royal Armouries, A3676(3), with thanks*)

about one hundred of the enemies had gathered themselves under a wall at Llanthony, upon whom wee discharged a demi-culvering, shot from the Barbican, which lighted in the midst of them, made the stones of the wall fly about their eares, and could not but doe good execution.[20]

For their part, the Royalists claimed to have 'dismounted' two of the city's guns on Saturday 19 August.

Table 1

Cannon	Bore (in)	Shot (lb)	Weight (lb)	Length (ft)	No. Oxen	Range (paces)	Range (metres)
Cannon Royal	8	64	8000	12	9	300 – 1500	200 – 1000
Cannon	7 $1/_4$	46 $3/_4$	6500	12	7	360 – 1740	240 – 1160
Demi-Cannon	6	24 $1/_2$	5000	11	5	340 – 1600	226 – 1066
Culverin	5 $1/_2$	19	4500	13 $1/_2$	4	420 – 2100	280 – 1400
Demi-Culverin	4 $1/_2$	11 $3/_4$	3000	11	4	380 – 1800	253 – 1200
Saker	3 $3/_4$	5 $1/_4$	1900	9 $1/_2$	3	300 – 1500	200 – 1000
Minion	3 $1/_4$	3 $1/_4$	1100	8	2	280 – 1400	186 – 933
Falcon	2 $3/_4$	3 $1/_3$	750	7	2	260 – 1200	173 – 800
Falconet	2 $1/_4$	1 $2/_7$	400	6	2	220 – 1000	146 – 666
Rabinet	1 $1/_2$	$3/_4$	300	5	2	150 – 700	100 – 466

Some of the types of cannon contained within the typical artillery train of the period. Figures vary and these should only be taken as averages. They are taken from Ward's *Animadversions of Warre*, with the addition of modern metric equivalents. The largest type that appears to have been used at Gloucester was a demi-cannon with a shot of 25 lb weight.

2) Digging of assault trenches – Saps

Once the defences were breached it was expected that troops would be able to pour in through the gap, having been brought up close in relative safety via 'saps'. These were trenches around 1 m wide and 1.2 m deep, used to approach the enemy ditch and try to drain it or fill it with faggots so that troops could pass across (usually protected by a timber and hide cover or mantlet) to either charge through an existing breach or to set explosives to undermine intact defences. References to the digging of trenches dominate the accounts of the fighting. 'Sapping' was one of the most dangerous

The art of seventeenth-century siege warfare, showing the use of saps and redoubts to attack a town. From *Les Travaux de Mars*. (*Andrew Saunders, with thanks*)

occupations in siege warfare. 'Digging-in' generally was not popular with the English army of the day and consequently was often used as a punishment. The trenches were dug on a zig-zag plan heading towards the city, linked one to another by communication trenches. The work was carried out by teams of men working one behind the other; each dug a short depth and then moved forwards, protected from opposing fire by a timber screen. Larger emplacements or 'redoubts' were dug at intervals to allow troops to assemble, and they might also contain artillery.

The Royalists lost no time in digging their earthworks. On the first night of the siege on 10 August they began making their artillery emplacements in Gaudy Green and outside the East Gate which were linked 'with a Trench all along and diverse works to maintain their men from beeing killed'.[21] The siegeworks were then extended northwards from the East Gate to the former north-east corner of the medieval defences. On 16 August 'the enemie began this day to intrench between Barton Street and the Fryar's barne, within muskety shot of the wals'.[22] (Musket range was about 100 m.) The nobility took their places in the trenches, for example Henry, Lord Spencer, wrote of the long times spent there (see Appendix 2). Prince Rupert had two narrow escapes: in the first he was

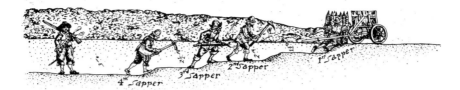

The manner of digging saps (in seventeenth-century style after the eighteenth-century illustration by Vauban). This was dangerous work although the sappers were given extra pay. It might also be used as a punishment duty

narrowly missed by a grenade (Tuesday 15 August) and in the second he was hit on his helmet by a stone from the walls (probably Monday 21 August).[23]

A breach had been made on the south-east corner of the defences (around what is now the junction of Parliament Street and Brunswick Road) within twenty-four hours of the start of the siege, although the defenders had been able to plug it with wool sacks and cannon baskets. A sap was dug up to the adjacent defence ditch which was then drained into a watercourse that ran into lower Southgate Street. Three days into the siege (13 August) the Royalists were making preparations to cross the ditch at this point and the constable of Barton Hundred demanded that thirty woodmen with tools should report to make faggots for filling in the ditch. There are numerous references thereafter to them bringing up faggots and soil to fill the ditch and to the defenders successfully driving them off by musket fire. By Saturday 26 August they had installed a mantlet to protect the work but this was repeatedly attacked with grenades. On the morning of Saturday 2 September the Royalists were well within pistol shot of the walls from this sap and must have been confident of a breakthrough at last, but the defenders were ready for them. Massey had cut a hole in the bottom of the defences from inside, presumably leaving a thin skin in place to conceal what they were doing until the last moment, and then at 8 a.m. he wheeled forward a 'sacre' (a 5–7 lb cannon) which fired bolt shot against the mantlet protecting the sappers. Bolt shot consisted of two balls linked by a chain, which could cut its way through the timber superstructure and blow away the cover. At the same time musketeers and grenadiers fired into the now-exposed trenches. Nevertheless, the Royalists still managed to advance towards the cannon which was consequently withdrawn in the evening and the hole then

'We battered their gallery with our
bolt shot.' Firing bolt shot at the
mantlet of the gallery being dug
towards the south-east corner of the
defences on 2 September

re-blocked. By the time that this story reached London it was reported that
Massey had brought forward six to seven cannon into this breach which were
loaded with musket balls ('case-shot') to blast the advancing troops

> and slew a great many of them, cutting them off as mowers cut
> grasse, and forced them to retreat, and in their retreat sallied out
> upon them, beat them out of their works, and took four carts laden
> with victuals from them.[24]

3) Mines
The principle of the mine was to dig under the defences, fill the shaft with
gunpowder and then explode the charge. The use of gunpowder in mines
had only recently been introduced to England in April 1643, when Prince
Rupert used the technique against Lichfield. At least three mines were
dug at the siege (according to the Royalist junior officer, Ensign John
Gwynne, in his *Military Memoirs*). One is referred to at the East Gate,
using miners pressed into service from the Forest of Dean. Some possible

evidence of this activity is represented by the discovery of a large, ill-defined, pit or ditch at least 9.5 m wide with late seventeenth-century material in the fill, observed in a watching brief on Wellington Street, 105 m outside the East Gate, in 1976.[25] This feature could have been part of the collapsed mine attacked by John Barnewood and his comrades on 1 September (see below). John Gwynne repeated a suggestion that the besiegers failed by dissipating their efforts over mining. He wrote

> I was at the siege of Gloucester, where then it was reported, that had there been as much care taken in making one mine ready, as in making of the other two which stayed for it, probably we had carried the town.[26]

DISPOSITION OF FORCES

No physical evidence now survives of this frenetic activity, but some information on the layout of the siegeworks can be mapped on the basis of the accounts by Dorney and Corbet, and using present topographical or archaeological evidence where possible. Such siegeworks were temporary and on a relatively small scale – and, therefore, easily destroyed. Many emplacements depended heavily on the portable 'gabions' and would leave no surface indication at all. Their short span of occupation also decreases the likelihood of the recovery of contemporary artefacts, so making accurate dating difficult. Within the excavated segments of the ditches and possible saps (see below) was found an overwhelming preponderance of residual material, derived from the Roman and medieval levels through which they were cut. The soil from these earlier periods had first been piled up as ramparts and then pushed back at the close of the siege.

The Royalist siegeworks were designed to provide a cover in depth and were particularly concentrated on the south and east sides where the main focus of any assault was clearly intended. Behind the forward trenches were artillery batteries, with troop concentrations further to the rear. Artillery batteries were built at Severn Street (now approximately the line of the entrance into the Docks from Southgate Street, 200 m from the defences), Gaudy Green and Rignall Stile off what is now Brunswick Road (120 m from the defences), and outside the East Gate. A substantial north to south ditch feature containing seventeenth-century tile, discovered

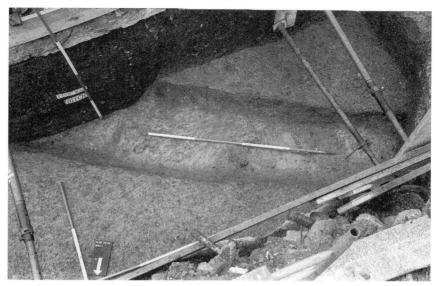

Excavation of the base of a Royalist sap on the Bank of England site, Southgate Street, during 1988. Scale in half metres. (*M. Atkin for Gloucester City Museums*)

during a watching brief at the junction of Cromwell Street and Park End Road, may represent the earthwork defences on the north side of the Rignall Stile battery.[27] These batteries were probably linked by a 'parallel' trench dug just in front, some small evidence of which was found 120 m outside the South Gate. There, on the Bank of England site, segments of two narrow trenches were found in 1988 (36/88.1). One was 1 m wide and flat-bottomed with the pattern of the fills, collapsing into the trench from the north, suggesting that there had originally been a bank on the north (city) side. It lay parallel to the city defences at a distance of 120 m (only 40 m from the point of the South Gate bastion) and may have been a communication trench, linking the Severn Street battery with that in Gaudy Green. The other trench, which ran at an angle, was 2.5 m wide and butt-ended and may have been a larger redoubt at the end of a sap.[28]

At a distance, beyond about 400 m, were the main camps of the Royalist army. The principal camps (leaguers) were at Llanthony, Barton Hill (cavalry) and, further to the rear, at Tredworth (400 m, 400 m and 1,000 m from the city, respectively). A section through the possible ditched earthwork on the city side of the Barton Hill cavalry quarters was

Part of the surviving buildings of Llanthony Priory – the site of one of the main Royalist camps at the siege. The tower of the former priory church was demolished before the siege to prevent it being used for artillery spotting by the Royalists

recorded on a watching brief as a 1 m wide and flat-bottomed ditch, of similar profile to the possible sap excavated on the Bank of England site, Southgate Street.[29] The ditch was cut through sand and its profile would therefore have been quickly eroded if it had been left open for any length of time (i.e. as a boundary ditch or drain). The only find from the feature was a mid seventeenth-century clay pipe bowl.

No evidence of the camp at Llanthony survives, although the troops presumably used the still-standing 'canon's lodge' and the medieval barn for shelter. In front of this camp was an artillery battery on Llanthony causeway, also 400 m from the city. The battery protected the main camp and could also provide enfilade fire along Gloucester quay. It has been located by reference to its siting 'in a field near Llanthony towards Severn, making a breast-work from it to Llanthony wall crosse the causey'.[30] Lysons states that the earthwork was 'perfectly visible' in 1860, 'extending from the old bridge over the Sudbrook, on the Hempsted and Gloucester road to the Severn'.[31] Nothing now remains.

There is less evidence for the disposition of forces to the north of the city. The Kingsholm battery was believed by Washbourn to have been located in former gravel quarries, about 280 m from the city defences and in front of a cavalry encampment at Walham. The forces from Worcester were reported as being quartered in Kingsholm 'in two fields there about, lesse than halfe a mile off us'.[32] From a combination of archaeological and early map evidence, it has been possible to equate these with two raised closes north of the land the city possibly stripped for its defences prior to the siege; they are defined on the west side by a ditch bounding Deans Way, on the south by a ditch fronting St Mark Street found in 1989[33] and by the parallel ditch along Edwy Parade (a former Roman defence ditch alignment used as a boundary of the later manor).[34] Further to the north, and east of the suspected site of the Walham encampment, on a watching brief during the Coppice Corner housing development, a number of musket balls, a small-bore cannon ball (Falconet: 474 gm/1 lb) and an archaic lance or pike head were found which *may* date to this period.[35] Further to the north-east, in 1991 a geophysical survey identified a rectangular, 30 m by 20 m, enclosure just below the crest of a slope overlooking the city and controlling the route along Horton Road between the documented camps at St Margaret's Hospital (attacked on 14 August) and Matson where the King was based. Limited trial trenching showed that this was defined by only a slight, 2 m wide by 0.20 m deep ditch with dating evidence from the seventeenth- or eighteenth-century date.[36] It may have been the remains of a Royalist observation post to contain the siege, possibly abandoned before completion.

SIEGE ENGINES

The city ditches presented a major obstacle to the besiegers. Sir Samuel Luke records that the Royalists brought up seven cartloads of ladders but one idea was to use specially-constructed siege engines that could drop bridges across them. Dr Chillingworth's siege engines were made up in the quarters of the Earl of Forth at Llanthony. Corbet described how

> They framed great store of those unperfect and troublesome engines to assault the lower parts of the city. Those engines ran upon wheels, with planks musket proof placed on the axel-tree, with holes for musket-shot and a bridge before it, the end whereof (the wheels falling into the ditch) was to rest upon our breast works.[37]

Later developments of the city defences were clearly designed to ensure that such devices could not work: 'To prevent this we intended to have made another ditch out of our workes, so that the wheels falling therein the bridge would have fallen too short of our brestworkes into our wet moat, and so frustrated their intentions'[38] (and see below, p. 129). As the engines were subsequently recovered by the citizens from the marsh on the south side of the town, they were presumably designed to cross the comparatively narrow (4 m) medieval trenches on that side where there was only an earthen rampart. It is hard to imagine them attempting to cross the wide ditches as constructed outside the South Gate. The scheme of defence shown on the 1780 Hall and Pinnell map can therefore be interpreted as a post-siege response to this threat. The failure of the siege engines is the generally-favoured explanation for the Humpty Dumpty rhyme, which in its early form reads thus:

> Humpety Dumpety fell in a beck,
> With all his sinews about his neck,
> All the King's surgeons and all the King's knights,
> Couldn't put Humpety Dumpety to rights [39]

The *beck* may refer to a stream or even to one of the ditches; the *sinews* may be the ropes that would have held the bridge; the reference to *surgeons* may be a reference to Chillingworth himself. Dr Chillingworth died in January 1644 after being captured at the siege of Arundel Castle.

OFFENSIVE DEFENCE

Massey knew that the best means of defence was, indeed, offence. He took much of the initiative during the siege by mounting raiding parties (sallies) and thereby distracting the Royalists from developing their plan of attack. This meant that Massey could concentrate his meagre forces where and when he wanted rather than simply spreading his men out along the defences and awaiting an assault. For the same reason he also used a simple form of psychological warfare to keep the besiegers on edge: 'it was the care of the governour to cause a perpetuall noise; that whensoever their cannon had been silent for awhile, one or two of our guns gave fire to disturbe the calm, and signifie to the country that we were yet alive'.[40]

This all bought valuable time while Parliament in London was desperately

'. . . severall sallies with small parties fell into the trenches, beate them out, gained some working tools, arms and prisoners . . .'. Some parts of the fighting had more in common with scenes from the western front in the First World War rather than the popular image of battles in the Civil War

trying to gather an army together to relieve the city. Massey also needed to keep up the morale of his unpaid troops, 'our men likewise were to be kept in the heat of action, to prevent the fainting of the spirits'.[41] This activity buoyed the spirits of the defenders, but it had a corresponding negative effect on the morale of the attackers. Corbet tells how

> As the soldiers within were heated with their own performance, so the enemy without, being wasted in a lingering design before the houre of service came, grew feeble in their own thoughts, and to us contemptible.[42]

Thus, much of the story of the siege is one of sallies and night-time raiding parties (see pp. 167–9). It is one of the ironies that it was the parliamentary defenders, usually led by the more experienced men of Stamford's regiment – men like Captain-Lieutenant James Harcus (see Appendix 2), or Captains Blunt, Gray or White who acted most in a 'cavalier' spirit. Corbet relates how 'our men from the walls could doe little to retard their pioners, but by severall sallies with small parties fell into their trenches, beate them out, gained some working tooles, arms and prisoners, and retreated without losse'.[43] The weapons and ammunition would have been particularly welcome supplies for the garrison. A parliamentary newspaper includes a graphic account of how

> the reports (but how certaine we know not) go thus, that the Souldiers of the City, leap over their own works and fall upon the Cavaliers in their Trenches, and knocke out their braines with the butt end of their muskets. That the Welch men brought lately to the Cavaliers, abundance of hay, straw and other Provisions for them to lie on, which the Garrison of the City perceiving issued out, beat the Cavaliers from their lodgings, fired the hay and straw, and so have forced them to lie on the bare and cold ground again.[44]

The Royalists had another answer to the mettle of the defenders – claiming that they were drunk! According to Clarendon, the prisoners that were taken confessed 'that the governor always gave the party that made the sally as much wine and strong water as they desired to drink – so that it seems their mettle was not purely natural'.[45] It is also possible that they had been smoking too much of the local tobacco which was of a variety (*Nicotiana Rustica*) that was hallucinogenic![46] These raids were not always successful. In that of 21 August, Henry Spencer says that they were 'well-beaten'. On the night of Wednesday 16 August, according to the *Memoirs of Prince Rupert,* there was a desperate sally at dusk on the camp at Llanthony and twenty-four 'Blue-coats' were left dead in one trench – 40 per cent of the city's total acknowledged losses.[47] (Both Stamford's regiment and the local militia wore blue coats, see below, p. 100.)

Snipers were also employed. On Thursday 31 August 'three of the company of Sergeant-Major Ferrer . . . crept along Seavern-Bank, and gave the enemy an alarm, holding them play almost an houre'. It is likely that they were used against the cannoneers, killing Berkeley and Scott on Saturday 19 August.[48] From elsewhere it is known that special fowling pieces with rifled barrels were used by snipers.

The raiding parties might consist of just a few men or could involve hundreds. The largest consisted of 400 musketeers, commanded by Major Pudsey and Captain Gray, when on the morning of Friday 18 August they

'. . . they left twenty-four blue-coats in one ditch, besides wounded men'. Not all of the
city sallies were successful. Both the Gloucester Trained Bands and the Earl of Stamford's
regiment wore blue coats

'Nailing' the cannon of the Royalist battery at Kingsholm on 18 August

sallied out of the North Gate to try to seize the four cannon recently
installed at Kingsholm. They got behind the battery defences with apparently only one shot being fired from the cannon. Both the Royalist and
City accounts admit that one cannon was indeed nailed, but the casualty
figures are at wide variance (see Table 2). The Royalist account describes
the to and fro of the battle as 'The rebels beat the Welsh out of the works,
and threw down part of them; but the Welsh retreating to the second
guard, both together returned and beat in the rebels'.[49] Another account of
this action tells of the Gloucester men using the butt-end of their muskets
to kill the enemy gunners.

Table 2

	City sources		Royalist sources	
Date	City Dead	Royalist Dead	City Dead	Royalist dead
Aug. 16	0	100 +	24	4
Aug. 18	2	104 +	27	11

One of the most complex actions occurred on the night of Monday 21 August when two assault groups attempted a pincer movement, working along the Royalist trenches. Unfortunately the plan failed because a confused local guide took the north party the wrong way and they ended up in Barton. Dorney describes how

> Two severall parties were designed for the nailing of the enemies canon. The one being about 200 musketeers . . . sallied forth at the North Gate to have fallen upon their trenches at the east gate, but their guide foolishly mistaking the way brought them round about to S. Jacob Ashley's quarters at Barton. . . . The other . . . sallied

'. . . sallied forth by boat downe Severne, and marched up to the enemies quarters at Severne Street'. The raid along Severn Street

forth by boat downe Severne, and marched up to the enemies quarters at Severne Street, beat the enemey out of their redoubt there . . .
and advance up to the turnpike at the upper end of Severn Street.[50]

Ashley (Astley) had based his camp at Wood's Mill on the River Twyver,
and Severn Street lies just off the line of the present entrance into the
Docks from Southgate Street. The north raiding party was drawn from the
Town regiment and Devereux's troops, while the south party came from
Lord Stamford's regiment. The Royalist account refers to the north party
being composed of 150 musketeers and 40 horse.

Such sallies, especially at night, would have quickly devolved into a
confused individual combat. Uniforms as such were not worn although
regiments were theoretically identifiable by the colour of their coats. Thus
troops of Merrick's regiment who had been in the garrison wore grey
coats, but unfortunately not only were the Gloucester Trained Bands and
Stamford's regiment issued with blue coats – but so also were part of the
King's army from Oxford! A common method of identifying friend or foe
was by simple badges (such as the sprig of greenery worn by the London

Reconstruction of the dress of a
musketeer of the Trained Bands. Most
of his equipment is perishable and
therefore does not survive well on
archaeological sites. (*M. Atkin, with
thanks to Mike Sims of the ECWS*)

Trained Bands who relieved Gloucester), or by ribbons in the hat or on the arm. Hence the messengers bringing the reply to the King's summons at the start of the siege put orange ribbons in their hats. At night such identification marks were of little value and the attackers might leave their shirt tails hanging out behind – hence a night assault was sometimes called a 'camisado' or 'shirt fight'.

The dreaded mines were dealt with in two ways, the first by direct assault. At 3 a.m. on Friday 1 September a small raiding party of five men slipped out of a sally port in the tower of the East Gate (which still survives) and crept towards the entrance to the mine being dug towards it. A hand-grenade was thrown in and those miners that survived the blast were shot down by musketeers as they ran out. The description tells how John Barnewood, a grenadier from the local militia (and indeed a manufacturer of grenadoes), and four comrades approached the mine and

> after he had taken aside the board that covered it, and a pretty while viewed them, fired and cast a granadoe in amongst them, our foure muskettiers playing at them as they ran out of it, and so retreated without harme. We killed foure and hurt others.[51]

'About three a clock in the morning, a sergeant and foure more of Captaine White's company, with one John Barnewood . . . crept forth of a hole made in the dungeon at the east gate . . .' Blocked medieval sally port in the south face of the south tower of the East Gate. It was probably this port that was referred to in the raid to ambush Royalist miners. (*Gloucester City Museums*)

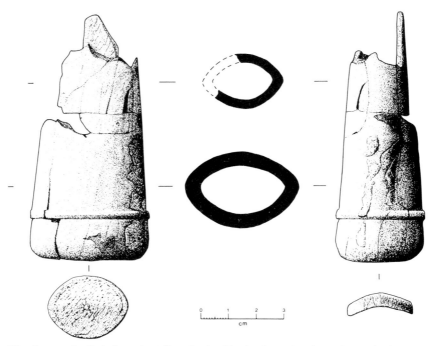

Wooden powder flask from site 36/88, Bank of England site, Southgate Street. Such perishable items rarely survive. (*D. Thomas*)

The second method consisted of digging counter-mines – with the prospect of fighting underground or having one's own tunnel blown up. On Monday 28 August 'We conceived that the enemy had sunke a mine under the east gate, whereupon we began to countermine in two severall places there, but finding springs we left off, conceiving the enemy would be forced to doe the like for the same reason'.[52] But the defenders miscalculated that the Royalists would be defeated by the high water table, for on 2 September, 'We discovered that the enemy, for all the springs, went on with their mine at the east gate, whereupon wee renewed our countermine there'.[53] They dug for the next two days and prepared large drills with which to bore down into their enemy's mine so that on 4 September:

This morning early our miners had gotten as far as the outward part of the East Gate, where by the working of the enemies we perceived their mine to be sunk a great deale lower than ours, so that we were

102

above them, whereupon we set workmen upon the making of great borers with which wee intended to bore through our mine into theirs, and so to drowne them the enemie's mine.[54]

Fortunately the siege was lifted before this plan had to be put into operation.

At this stage – at the end of August and the first week of September – there are a number of signs that the fighting was getting more desperate as both sides sensed that the final assault was near. A new battery was under construction outside the East Gate; the defenders realized that the Royalists were digging mines there and the sap at the south-east corner was getting dangerously close to the city wall. Some stories of the siege did reach London at this time and feature Massey taking a more direct part in proceedings. This may have simply been propaganda for the benefit of a London audience in need of a hero (as such direct involvement is not mentioned by Dorney, who was careful to list the commanders of the other sallies), but it may also reflect Massey's concern to rally his troops for the expected final assault. A report from messengers from Gloucester to London in early September tells how on 29 August

> the enemy by a very desperate assault against part of the outworks on Tuesday made a great breach in the breast work, and drew up three peeces of ordnance into the breach, and went about to cast up a half-moon. But the governor sallying forth of the town beat them back from all their advantages, made good the breach, took their three peeces of ordnance, and forced them to leave a fourth behind them in the field . . . as near as can be imagined the enemy lost above 500 men in this day's service, and the town but 16.[55]

This seems to have been a grossly exaggerated version of the attack on the south-east corner as reported by Dorney and possibly refers to a glacis bank on the outer side of the ditch.

The attempted storming of defended towns was, indeed, one of the bloodiest aspects of the fighting in the Civil War.

PROPAGANDA

Words also became an important weapon in the Civil War. It was not a war in the medieval vein when people blindly followed their feudal lords;

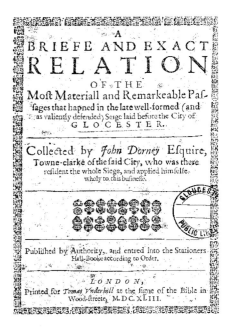

A

BRIEFE AND EXACT
RELATION
OF THE
Moſt Materiall and Remarkeable Paſ-
ſages that hapned in the late well-formed (and
as valiently defended) Seige laid before the City of
GLOCESTER.

Collected by *John Dorney* Eſquire,
Towne-clarke of the ſaid City, who was there
reſident the whole Siege, and applied himſelfe
wholy to this buſineſſe.

Publiſhed by Authority, and entred into the Stationers
Hall-Booke according to Order.

LONDON,
Printed for *Tomas Vnderhill* at the ſigne of the Bible in
Wood-ſtreete, M.DC.XLIII.

Books were weapons during the Civil War
and served a valuable propaganda
function. John Dorney wrote possibly the
most valuable account of the siege soon
after the events themselves. (*Glos. Colln,
Gloucester City Library, with permission*)

ordinary folk were very aware of the issues that were involved. To a great
extent this change was due to a combination of increasing literacy and the
collapse of censorship, consequently leading to the tremendous flood of
publications of sermons, speeches and newsbooks that characterized the
period. Such publications were not always treated with the respect their
authors believed that they deserved. The dispirited writer of the new
Profitable Intelligencer in London complained that after only a week the
newsheets were 'carelessly hurled up and down, and sometimes torn in
pieces to light tobacco, and other uses not fit to be named'.[56]

The newsbooks were propaganda mouthpieces and could both promote
and counter the rumours that abounded. There were fears in London during October 1642 that the Royalists had actually seized control of
Gloucester. On 4 October Lord Grandison was reported as being in
Gloucester with 2,000 men who were plundering the county around, but
there is no other confirmation that this story was true.[57] To ensure that
such a rumour was quashed, it appears that Parliament may have produced
a spurious account of a battle in which the non-existent Royalist army was
defeated by an equally non-existent parliamentary force of 2,500 men, with

a 'bloudy battaile' on 11 October.[58] At the end of August 1643 further rumours were spread among the prison ships in London holding Royalist prisoners that Gloucester had actually fallen in the siege.[59] Victories were exaggerated and defeats dismissed. At the start of the siege the Royalist *Mercurius Aulicus*, writing from Oxford, described the burning of the Gloucester suburbs as 'surely is not to keepe the city either for the King or Parliament . . . I dare promise you (God willing) a very speedy account of the siege of Gloucester'. Arguments over casualty figures in the siege, with the city claiming a Royalist loss of 1,500 and the Royalists only admitting to 100, have a very modern ring. Propaganda could also spread useful misinformation. *Mercurius Aulicus* claimed to have intercepted a letter from London at the start of the siege stating 'Gloucester cannot be relieved' and later went on to cast scorn on the 'fine new fictions' of the parliamentary newspapers. These included the claim that Massey had tricked eight troops of Royalist cavalry into entering an open gate but had then trapped them inside ('a very pretty story; 'tis pitty it is a lie'). In an interesting example of the way in which a story could change, the first account of the desertion of the cannoneer Hatton, written during the siege itself (probably by Dorney), describes how he had been captured after an unlikely attempt to swim the River Severn in order to recover his strayed horse![60] By September, after the immediate need to stress unity had passed, Hatton was more honestly being described as a rogue deserter.[61]

CHAPTER 6

Inside the Besieged City

But for your bug-beare threats so huge and big,
If seven score cannons can but kill one pig,
We then have cause to fear nothing but sin
Can make a breach to let such Rebels in

FROM 'AN EPIGRAM UPON TWO LAWYERS, BELL AND HILL, WHO WERE SENT
INTO GLOCESTER TO PERSWADE THEM TO YEELD'

With the exception of the razing of the suburbs (used to demonstrate the dedication of the citizens), the parliamentary commentators played down the damage done by the siege in order to ridicule the efforts of the attackers, although after the war the total cost was claimed as being over £34,000.[1] Great play was made of the death of a pig by a spent cannon-shot as being one of the limits of serious injury.[2]

However, the siege did undoubtedly cause hardship. One of the first actions of the Royalists was to cut off the city water supply, by cutting the lead pipes carrying the water from the springs on Robinswood Hill. They also diverted the water that drove the city corn mills on the River Twyver. Consequently the city had to rely on wells and water from the River Severn, and had to grind their corn with horse mills. Supplies of fuel were also cut off and this may have driven the inhabitants to collect turf to dry as a substitute. Otherwise the city appears to have had sufficient warning to ensure that it was well supplied (partly from seizing the crops of Royalist gentry on the Cotswolds). It was able to continue to graze its cattle and the Epigram above refers to 'We having beefe, they eating cabidge all'.

Part of the Royalist tactic was to attempt to fire the city using mortars and red-hot shot but this seems to have been unsuccessful. Dorney describes an early incident (17 August) when the Royalists shot 'divers genadoes out of their battery in Gawdy Green into the towne; whereof about four fell upon some houses, and brake into them, but (by God's providence) did no harm'.[3] Corbet also tells how they

> dayly acted to the terrour of the inhabitants; shooting grenadoes, fire-bals, and a great stones out of their mortar pieces. . . . Thence in one night they shot above twenty fiery melting hot iron bullets . . . which were seen to fly through the ayre like the shooting of a starre. They passed through stables, and ricks of hay, where the fire by the swiftness of the motion did not catch, and falling on the tops of the houses, presently melted the leads, and sunk through; but all the skill and industry of the enemy could not set one house on fire.[4]

According to the parliamentary press only one woman and three others were killed by the barrage, none were maimed and only a few were slightly hurt.[5] Corbet states that the grenadoes were 'guided by the hand of

Greyfriars was used as a command post by Col. Massey during the siege; it was ideally placed behind the main crisis points of the East and South Gates and the south-east corner. It was severely damaged by artillery during the fighting and is now a ruin

providence into by-places'.[6] On 19 August the Royalists fired over 150 cannon balls into the city. However, the batteries were so close that, according to Corbet, if the shot missed the wall it flew right over the town. Thus the cannon fire 'by such slender execution became so contemptible that at that very time women and children wrought hard in lining the walls and repairing the breaches'.[7]

One house that was hit was No. 30 Westgate Street, belonging to Mr Commeline, a local apothecary, on 25 August. The shot

> came through three houses and fell into a chamber of Mr Comelines the apothecary, and being perceived, many payles of water were cast upon it to quench the same, but that little availing, it was cast into a cowle of water, where after a good space it cooled.[8]

Such difficulty in burning the houses must be contrasted with the apparent ease with which the citizens had earlier managed to raze the suburbs and the other well-attested cases of post-medieval fires in English cities. It may well be that many of the houses in the suburbs were cheaper and 'unmodernized' thatched-roofed buildings, whereas it is clear that those in the city had been more extensively rebuilt with lead, stone slate and tile roofs that would not burn so easily.

Nevertheless, St Katherine's church (formerly St Oswald's priory on the north side of the city) was destroyed and the former Greyfriars towards the south-east corner was badly damaged by the battery. The South Gate was so badly damaged that it had to be pulled down (to be rebuilt in 1644). The top of the steeple of St Nicholas's church on Westgate Street was also destroyed and the Tolsey at The Cross damaged.[9] One cannon ball fell near The Catherine Wheel public house on Berkeley Street and demolished a brick wall. But it is significant that no claims for internal damage were made to the 1646 Grand Inquest and claims were couched in only general terms in the plea to Parliament in 1651.[10] Other damage seems almost apocryphal: a sundial marks the place where a cannon ball is reputed to have struck St Mary de Crypt on Southgate Street – the church was the site of the main ammunition magazine. Another lucky hit from a culverin was to The Crown Inn (Massey's lodging) on Westgate Street (No. 85) when, on 24 August, 'One bullet of about twenty pound weight came through a chamber of the inne called the Crowne, carried a boulster before it into the window, and there slept in it'.[11]

A sundial on the south buttress of the chancel of St Mary de Crypt is reputed to mark the spot where a cannon ball struck the church

By 5 September, although the store of ammunition was running dangerously low, food was still apparently plentiful.[12] The continuation of normal life through the short period is not something that archaeology can easily demonstrate in a positive sense. For instance, if people were worried enough to bury hoards of coins during the siege, their success meant that then they were equally able to recover them afterwards – and so leave no physical trace of any temporary panic. (By contrast, a carefully-prepared hoard of 309 coins, having a face value of £17 13s 6d and with a suggested date of 1643, was found in 1981 at Weston-sub-Edge, west of Evesham.[13])

CHILDREN AT WAR

Then, as now, war was no respecter of age and children played an active role in the siege. The earliest reported casualties in the siege were a boy and girl 'through their indiscetion gazing over the walles'.[14] Children helped in the construction and repair of the defences as 'All suspended

The Civil War was
no respecter of age.
Children in
Gloucester
laboured to make
the defences, spied
and even fought

private cares, and the women and children acted their parts in making up
the defects of the fortifications'.[15] Some even took part in the fighting. On
9 August a raiding party went out of the North Gate towards Barnwood,
and included a little boy of Captain Nelme's company from the Town
regiment who, having used all his bullets, 'charged his musket with a pebble stone, and killed a commander therewith'.[16] One boy acted as a spy,
bringing a message from London to warn of the impending departure of
the Earl of Essex's army. He then took advantage of a sally to infiltrate a
party of retreating Royalists and get back into the Royalist lines – claiming
to be an escaped prisoner from the city – and after being fêted for the
evening, slipped back to London the next day.[17] For some the strain
became too much and one 'little boy' is described as having deserted to the
enemies' trenches.

Lower leg-bone of a cow with a pebble embedded in it, found in seventeenth-century levels just outside the Outer North Gate (Horse and Groom site). This is possibly from a young beast which was accidentally hit by a pebble fired from a musket during the siege, while grazing in the nearby meadows. (*M. Atkin for Gloucester City Museums*)

CHAPTER 7

The Relief of the City

Thy right hand, O Lord, is become glorious in power.
Thy right hand, O Lord, has dashed in pieces the enemy.

EXODUS 15, v. 67

This was the verse that Sergeant Foster chose to begin his story of the Relief of Gloucester and the march of the Earl of Essex's army that culminated in the battle of Newbury.[1] For the men of Parliament, God was clearly on their side.

There is a discrepancy as to how much warning Massey may have had regarding the arrival of Essex's army. Corbet states 'The straitness of the siege debarred all intelligence', while Clarendon held that Massey 'found means to send many messengers out of the town, to advertise the straits he was in, and the time that he should be able to hold out'.[2] Two spies were sent out to get confirmation of the London boy's story (see p. 111) from Warwick – other messengers apparently having failed to get through there before. One of them, Thomas Prince, was described as 'creeping on his belly through the King's army, to make known the state of things in Gloucester'. In return, John Bridges at Warwick Castle had been able to pass on to these two 'substantial men' a message from the Earl of Essex explaining the reason for the delay in departure of the relief army.[3] Thus, on Thursday 24 August (two days before the relief army actually set forth), a fire was lit on Wainlode Hill (on the road to Tewkesbury). Although somewhat premature, this would at least warn the citizens that plans to relieve them were at last being finalized. Bridges was also able to pass back to Essex the latest information as to the poor morale of the Royalist besiegers. The Royalists had evidently heard the same stories of an impending relief army, but Massey was not fooled when Col. Gerard staged a mock skirmish, with troops supposedly from the relief army on

St Mary's church, Painswick, was used as a prison for captured parliamentarians. One, Richard Foot, carved an apt quotation within the church 'Be bold, be bold, but not too bold' (from Spenser's *Faerie Queen*). In 1644 there was a skirmish here and Gloucester troops were besieged in the church until forced to surrender to Vavasour's Royalists. The latter used two culverins in the mini-siege. There are reputedly marks of shot on the north side of the tower and on the east end of the church

Churchdown Hill at midnight on Friday 25 August, and lit fake warning fires. The news that it was to be Essex who was to command the relief army did not seem to engender much confidence in Gloucester. Corbet tells that the two spies returned to the city and brought the news of the advance of Essex 'who then lay under a cloud, [and] did give no great assurance'. On the night of Sunday 3 September two more men were sent out to light fires if they received further reports of Essex's army.

The meagre reports that went into the *Perfect Diurnal* and other parliamentary newspapers in London, exaggerated and even invented as some were, played an important role in maintaining the interest of the capital in the events in the west – ultimately ensuring the relief of the city. The fact that the Speaker of the House of Commons was William Lenthall, the Recorder of Gloucester (an MP for Oxfordshire), would also undoubtedly have helped their cause. The people of London were made to feel that their fate was very much bound up in the ability of Gloucester to resist and so prevent a rapid march on the capital by the Royalists. It was better to defend London in Gloucestershire rather than at the gates of the capital itself! So the capital frantically organized the relieving force which

'Lobster Pot' cavalry helmet found at Manor Farm, Quedgeley. This is a poor quality English copy of the continental Zischagge type of helmet, characterized by the fluted skull and the single nasal bar. Unlike the continental examples, however, the skull is made up of two plates riveted along the crown rather than being of a single piece; whilst the neck guard is made from a single plate of metal rather than constructed from articulated lames. The ring on the top was to allow the helmet to be suspended from the saddle. This type tended to be used by the Royalists (who had to rely more on imported weapons and armour than the parliamentary forces). (*P. Greatorex for Gloucester City Museums*)

eventually left under the Earl of Essex. It had to be paid for by a compulsory loan equivalent to fifty times the current subsidy rate. By 21 August they had raised three new auxiliary regiments to add to three existing regiments of the Trained Bands (around five thousand men in all to add to Essex's army of ten thousand). The 'Committee for militia for the relief of Gloucester' also ordered the shutting-up of shops until Gloucester was relieved as a gesture of solidarity and to free more of the workforce for the relief army.[4]

The Earl of Essex's relief army mustered on 24 August and set off on 26 August. Essex declared the day before that 'I am tomorrow god willing beginning my march, and if the army be as willing to march as I shall be to lead them and the town should wait until we can relieve them, I shall endeavour it, or perish in the act'.[5]

Travelling in a number of columns scattered across the countryside, it
finally marched down Prestbury Hill on 5 September and quartered in
Cheltenham before reaching Gloucester itself on 8 September. However,
the Royalist army had already withdrawn to avoid battle – first to
Painswick and thence to Sudeley Castle. For the city, the first clear sign
that the siege was about to end was on 4 September when they could see
the Royalists loading their sick on to boats to take them to Bristol and the
Royalist cavalry withdrawing from around Gloucester. On the following
day the citizens saw carriages pulling out of the Llanthony camp and moving across Tredworth Field and

> we perceived their foote and horse marching after, yet we were not
> assured of their raysing of their seige, or that reliefe was so nere at
> hand, till we perceived their rere guard to fire their hutts, and their
> men to be drawn out of their trenches . . .[6]

The siege was over! Part of the reason for the slowness of the march was
that Essex refused Parliament's urging to leave behind his heavier cannon.[7]
Carlyle later gave begrudging praise for the enterprise.

> The steady march to Gloucester and back again, by Essex, was the
> chief feat that he did during the war; a considerable feat, and very
> characteristic of him, the slow-going, inarticulate, indignant, some-
> what elephantine man.[8]

Why Did the Siege Fail?

The Royalists had not expected Parliament to have been able to raise such
a large force and certainly not so soon. Early reports of the movement of
Essex's army were met with disbelief. Plans for a final assault on the city,
based on the preceding artillery barrage, mines and sapping, were probably only just coming to fruition as the imminent approach of Essex's army
was announced. The average length of a siege during the Civil War (dis-
counting that of Basing House) was forty-three days and Gloucester was
relieved after only twenty-five. It seems very likely that the city may have
fallen within the next week, as supplies of ammunition were exhausted,
and breaches were completed at the East Gate and along the south wall.

The Earl of Essex's relief army marched down from the Cotswolds in battle order, eight hundred to a thousand men abreast and six lines deep. (*Richard Ellis for Devereux's Regiment of the ECWS*)

Nevertheless, this was still a longer period than the Royalists had expected the city to hold out for. Clarendon recalled how, after the King returned to Oxford (after the battle of Newbury), 'The siege of Gloucester was not believed to have been well conducted, and that it might have been taken in half the time they were before it, if it had been skillfully gone about'. Scapegoats were sought as 'this clamour against that engagement was so popular and universal, that no man took upon himself to speak in defence of it'.[9] And so they 'looked upon that undertaking at Gloucester, as the ruin of the King's affairs'.[10] Clarendon (writing of events a few months later) was particularly scathing over the qualities of leadership of Lord Ruthven.

The General, though he had been without doubt a very good officer, and had great experience, and was still a man of unquestionable courage and integrity; yet he was now much decayed in his parts, and with the long continued custom of immoderate drinking, dozed in his understanding, which had been never quick and vigorous; he having been always illiterate to the greatest degree that can be imagined. . . . He was a man of few words, and of great compliance, and usually delivered that as his opinion, which he foresaw would be grateful to the King.[11]

Nevertheless, the first cause of failure was probably King Charles's desire to spare the city an outright attack in the first days. Thereafter morale deteriorated. *Certain Informations* tells of Royalist cavalry having to force the infantry to attempt to assault a breach and how this led to the Royalists fighting among themselves, and it is possible that there was at least an element of truth in this story.[12] The draft account of the siege written before it ended (and probably by Dorney) includes a story that 'There was a speach among the Common Souliers they should have orders to Martch away, butte there next orders was a rigment of horse irvironed them in, and kept Sentry all thatt night'.[13]

But Essex's army should never have been allowed to reach Gloucester. Clarendon claimed that on the onset of the march, the Royalists had not believed that Essex was seriously attempting to reach Gloucester, but rather that he was making a feint to Oxford with the idea of tempting the besieging army away from Gloucester in order to protect their headquarters. Otherwise Essex must pass through wasted countryside where he could not find supplies and eventually arrive at Gloucester where his tired forces could be easily cut off and destroyed. Thus it was a march

> where half the King's body of horse would distress, if not destroy his whole army, and through a country eaten bare, where he could find neither provision for man nor horse; and if he should, without interruption, be suffered to go into Gloucester, he could neither stay there, nor possibly retire to London, without being destroyed in the rear by the King's army . . .[14]

Sergeant Foster tells of his comrades spending days without food and not being able to light fires on the cold nights; where men would run half a mile or more on the rumour of there being water ahead. What kept them going, according to Foster, was their belief in the just cause, sure in the faith that 'the Lord that called us to do the work enabled us to undergo such hardships as He brought us to'.[15]

The Royalist plan had been to harry the relieving force along its route of march, so that it would not have been in a position to stand up against the King's army when it finally arrived at Gloucester, and could then have been decisively beaten. But the Royalist cavalry under Lord Wilmot was accused of cowardice in falling back before Essex's army rather than in engaging it. The most serious attempt to halt the march was not until 4 September when Prince Rupert attempted to cut off the London Trained Bands near Chipping Norton with a force of around four thousand horse, but he failed. By the time that the army reached Stow-on-the-Wold on the same day, the various columns of the relief army had all come together and were marching in battle order on the Swedish model – eight hundred to a thousand men abreast and six lines deep. It must surely have been an impressive sight but if they were expecting to actually come to battle then they were to be disappointed – Rupert's cavalry fell back while skirmishing along the front of the line of march. Charles felt it was too much of a gamble to bring Essex to battle there and then, and risk a pincer movement from both Essex and the city, and consequently pulled back his forces with the hope of fighting Essex in open country. Essex was no doubt heartily relieved; his men were exhausted and starving. Clarendon wrote scathingly after the war:

> The not engaging the earl of essex in all the march over so open a country, was thought unexusable, and was imputed to the want of courage in Wilmot, whom Prince Rupert did in no degree favour: nor was the Prince himself without some reproaches, for suffering the earl of essex, after all the horse was joined, to march down a long steep hill into the vale of Gloucester, without any disturbance; and that the whole army, when it was found necessary to quit the siege, had not been brought to fight in that vale, and at some distance from the town, when the King's men were fresh, and the other side tired with so long a march.[16]

Both the Royalist and parliamentary press then accused the other side of refusing to come to a decisive battle. This decision was defended by the Royalist *True and Impartiall Relation of the Battaile* in claiming that the King was being shrewd keeping his advantage over choosing the battleground:

Seventeenth-century glove, reputed to be that of Charles I and left at Matson House as a keepsake. (*P. Greatorex for Gloucester City Museums*)

the earl of Essex having descended with his army into the vale of Gloucester, before the King could well draw his from the siege up to the hills to fight with him, it was not thought fit to follow him into the inclosed country, where the King should loose the great advantage hee had above him in these three ends: to accomodate his quarters; to strengthen him in provisions; and equally to intercept his flight in a faire country.[17]

For Gloucester, to be relieved at all was enough – for the moment. Essex was presented with a hogshead of claret and a half hogshead of sack as a token of their thanks. As for Massey – he was awarded £1,000 by Parliament and recommended to Essex for promotion (which did not materialize). The arrears of the garrison were also ordered to be paid, and the officers and men were to receive one month's pay as a reward for their endeavours.[18] The initial euphoria was, however, tempered by the long delay in carrying out such fine sentiments.

CHAPTER 8

War Continues
1644–51

The drama of the 1643 siege creates a natural tendency to assume that all evidence of seventeenth-century defences must relate to the siege itself, but this was only one part of the story of Gloucester's involvement in the Civil War.

The Earl of Essex's army returned to London, but there was fierce periodic fighting around Gloucester throughout 1644–5, as the Royalists, first under Vavasour and then Col. Mynne, with an army of around six thousand men, tried to mount a remote blockade based on garrisons in the surrounding towns and villages. Massey countered by installing his own outer garrisons, spreading his meagre forces dangerously thin.[1]

PAYING THE TROOPS

The most immediate need in September 1643 was to pay the arrears owing to the garrison – owed £8,000 according to Royalist accounts.[2] They had proved loyal during the siege but had been mutinous before it and were likely to be so again. Tensions boiled over on 4 August 1644 when there was an argument between two of Massey's senior officers – Sergeant-Major Gray and Major Hammond – during a Council of War. Gray struck Hammond and they went outside to fight a duel. Gray was killed by a wound to the neck and the other officers 'fell quite off the hinges'. Massey cooled the situation by sending Hammond's men out on a sortie while Hammond himself was arrested. He was later acquitted on the grounds of self-defence.[3] In January 1645 officers came to Massey to resign their commissions so that they could 'seek their livelihood and advancement in other parts, where better provision and entertainment is made for the soldiery'. There had indeed been mutinies and some soldiers had been executed.[4] By February the situation was so bad that Massey wrote 'the fear of the enemy is nothing to our officers in comparison of the dread of having their throats cut by our own soldiers now their pay has failed them'.[5] Massey put part of the blame for the state of affairs on Thomas Pury, accusing him of trying to form his own party with the disgruntled troops.

A deputation was sent to Parliament asking for more troops and money. Both requests were formally acceded to, but it is not clear how much of this money actually reached the city. Some funds were provided for by confiscating the estates of Sir Richard Ducie and Sir Edward Hales, and later Sir Francis Willoughby, but Massey never received the £10,000 he had asked for, and the continuing problems of funding the garrison became increasingly rancorous. At one point Massey was billeting sixty soldiers and a troop of horse at his own expense. The problems were not helped in January 1645 by a Major Ingoldsby (or Inglesby) taking money intended to be used to raise horse and then disappearing from the city with fifteen horses, men and arms.[6]

IMPROVEMENT OF THE DEFENCES

Little time was lost after the siege in levelling Royalist earthworks and in completing and improving the defences against possible renewed attack. On 18 September a committee was appointed to 'see to the amending and reparation of all places defective in the wall and works round about the city and for cleansing of the ditches and perfecting of such works as are already begun'.[7] The cost of repairing the defences around the East Gate was 14d per perch and the labourers were paid up to 1s per day – the work included the repair of holes in the wall blasted by the cannon fire.[8] The mine shafts were also demolished and the timber used elsewhere.[9] Such 'cleansing' has, of course, removed much of the likely artefactual evidence for the siege. In February 1644 Captain Backhouse described the 'sconces' at the East and North Gates and one at Friar's Orchard (on the south-east corner) as still being unfinished. How much remained to be achieved is clear from the financial accounts and ordinances detailing further work needed upon them. In 1644 the Quarter Sessions ordered that all tenants should work at the fortifications at the rate of one day's work for every yard of land that they occupied. Samuel Baldwin, the man responsible for

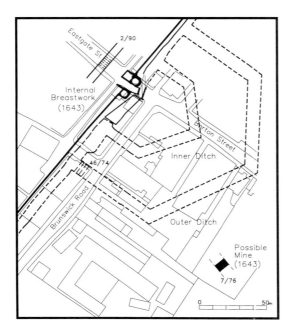

Plan of the 1644–51 bastion outside the East Gate, also showing the internal retrenchment and possible mine dug in 1643. Based on the results of watching briefs and the Hall and Pinnell map

rebuilding the South Gate in 1644, was appointed General Surveyor of the City Works in December 1644.[10] Massey continued to press for more men and supplies, and in March 1644 it was Oliver Cromwell, then still only a colonel, who was charged with guarding ammunition at Warwick that was destined for Gloucester.[11]

HARRYING THE ROYALISTS

The main strategy of late 1643–5 was to harass the enemy so that they could not build up strength and close in for a siege. It was perhaps during this phase of the operation that Massey showed his tactical skill to best advantage. This was a campaign fought in the taking and retaking of small garrisons based on small towns and country houses. Sir John Wyntour now started to play a notable part in the proceedings in establishing his Royalist garrisons in the Forest of Dean. In the space of five months from November 1643 Massey was in action at Tewkesbury, Berkeley, Beverstone, Brockthorpe, Cheltenham, Chepstow, Hartpury, Highleaden, Huntley, Marshfield, Newent, Painswick, Taynton, Tetbury

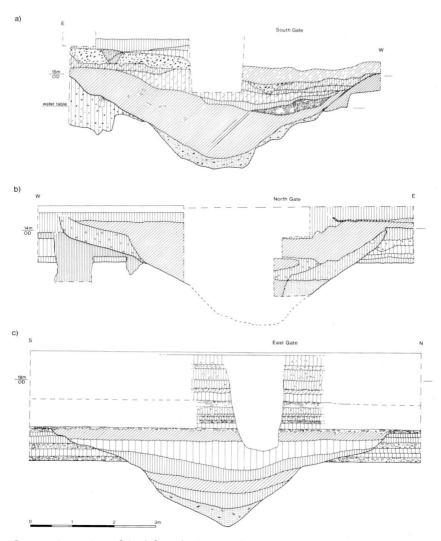

Comparative sections of the defence ditches recorded outside a) the South Gate and b) the outer North Gate, both dating to 1643 and c) the East Gate dating to 1644–5; a) is from an excavation in 1983; b) and c) are from watching briefs. *(From field drawings by C. Guy and A.P. Garrod)*

and Wotton-under-Edge, and further afield at Malmesbury (Wiltshire). Some idea of the pressure that he managed to maintain on the Royalists in the district is well illustrated by his campaigns in May 1644. On 7 May Massey set off with a force to attack the Royalist garrison at Mr Colchester's house in Westbury. The pamphlet *Ebenezer* claimed that he had 900 foot and a regiment of horse together with Col. Purefoy's cavalry and two cannon. Having seized that he sent the cavalry on to take Little Dean and on the next day he took Newnham. There, after storming the defences, Massey's men followed the retreating Royalists into the church. Although most of the Royalists then called out to surrender, one of Sir John Wyntour's servants – called Tipper – decided to take as many of the enemy with him as possible and attempted to blow up a barrel of gunpowder. This failed but naturally angered the attackers 'which occasioned the putting of more to the sword than otherwise had been'. Massey then moved on to Lydney. Here, finding the defences of Wyntour's headquarters too strong for the limited force that he had brought with him, he satisfied himself by burning three iron mills. They then moved straight away to Ross-on-Wye where they seized Wilton Bridge. Massey finally returned to Gloucester on 21 May but left again the very next day, gathered his forces together in Ross and marched on Beverstone Castle, 15 miles (24 km) to the south of Gloucester. This fell on 23 May and led to the comment, 'he loves to be in action, and is now trying experiments every day, and his soldiers do exceedingly rejoice in his actings and exposings'.[12] Still not satisfied, Massey decided to go further afield and stormed Malmesbury in Wiltshire on 25 May.

Apart from the direct military value of not allowing the Royalists to consolidate their hold on the county, they also served to keep his discontented, unpaid, troops occupied. For this reason the seizure of provisions was just as valuable – 'he had also taken a barge of the enemy's upon the river of the Severne laden with sacke, tobacco, and ammunition going from Worcester' in January 1644.[13]

But Massey did not have things all his own way. In August 1644, Mynne's troops were within a quarter of a mile (0.4 km) of Gloucester as they ran off cattle and threatened to burn the harvest. In the spring of 1645 the Royalists plundered Winchcombe, but nowhere suffered greater than the Forest of Dean. Wyntour began establishing garrisons based on the country houses there soon after the siege of Gloucester was lifted and these were taken and retaken over the next eighteen months. Wyntour relied heavily on troops brought from Monmouthshire and Herefordshire and in March 1645 a reinforcement of 3,500 men came from Prince Rupert. The Royalist army of Prince Rupert entered the Forest in April 1645 and newsbooks report that in some parishes every building was burnt down as they tried to clear Massey's garrisons. Massey was able to do little to intervene at that time and many of the population were forced to hide in the mines. Others 'now resolved (since all is gone) to make the warre their living' – whether they meant by this that they would join the army or simply resort to banditry is not clear. Soon after, Massey's force faced near fatal disaster as Prince Rupert attacked them at Ledbury. Massey had his horse killed under him – reputedly by the Prince himself. The House of Commons seemed so relieved by Massey's survival (despite the loss of over two hundred men) that they granted him £200, the iron works and mills of Sir John Wyntour and six equipped horses.[14] This was the low point of his fortunes but his seizure of Evesham in June 1645 enabled him to leave his command at Gloucester to Col. Walter Lloyd (shortly replaced by Col. Thomas Morgan) with the city safe. The Gloucester forces under Morgan were then involved in the last battle of the First Civil War on 21 March 1646 when Sir Jacob Astley's army was defeated at Stow-on-the-Wold.

'DIRTY TRICKS'

The 'dirty tricks' war also continued. The most famous conspiracy at the time was the Backhouse Plot. In November 1643, Captain Backhouse (on Massey's staff) was offered a royal pardon if he would betray the city, but he informed Massey and the two of them planned a double-cross. The plan was that Backhouse would pretend to persuade Massey to divert a large part of the Gloucester garrison into mounting an attack elsewhere (Berkeley Castle was suggested). He would then dupe Sir William Vavasour into thinking he had arranged an easy access for the Royalists via the West Gate. The reality was that Massey would be waiting with additional cannon and grenadiers at the West Gate, and with men posted under Over Bridge ready to collapse it, thus trapping the Royalists between the river and the city. The complicated manouvrings continued until February, with negotiations with the Royalists to make them fall in with the plan. Eventually it failed and the Commons published a full account in May 1644.[15]

THIRD CIVIL WAR

There were renewed, feverish, preparations for defence in 1650–1 before the defeat of Charles II at the battle of Worcester on 3 September 1651. Now a Royalist (see Appendix 1), Massey was leading the advance guard of the King's army on its march from Scotland, and Gloucester was seen as an obvious target for him. In 1650, £600 from the Excise Duties was spent on renewing the defences and 80 tons of timber were ordered to be provided by the 'preservators' of the Forest of Dean to repair the artillery platforms.[16] The latter were the rafts of timbers used to provide a firm footing for the cannon on top of the earth ramparts. With the arrival of Charles II's Scottish army in Worcester it appeared that Gloucester was once more in danger. Some of the parliamentary troops had indeed retreated there. Lieutenant General Fleetwood wrote that 'M.G. Massey marches with a party to Glocester, in hopes that upon his approach his old friends will appear for him'.[17] There was a renewed urgency in the defence works. On 23 August 1651 £7 was distributed to the fourteen companies of foot of the city 'for their extraordinary labour in the fortifications of this garrison for two daies and two nights past'.[18] A letter from Mayor Anthony Edwards to the Speaker of Parliament on 23 August describes how they 'every day and sometime in the night laboured to repair all the Bullwarkes and fortifications' which were described as ruinous.[19] On 20 August, 'All the draught-horses in and about the city prest to hawl timber for the breast-work upon the quay'.[20] On 25 August 1651 'all burgesses and inhabitants of Glocester, who are not listed, are to muster by themselves, servants or workmen tomorrow morning by six o'clock, with spades, shovels and mattocks and little baskets at the south gate, to work at the fortifications all that day upon pain of 5s a piece'.[21] This was presumably to clean out the ditches and carry out repairs but soil was also being imported to strengthen the ramparts. An order given to repair the south defences included plough teams so that

> turf be forthwith digged and cutt out of the pasture round called 'The Causeway ground' otherwise 'the Bell ground' lying between the high orchard and the high causeway leading to Llanthony, and that teemes and plowes be forthwith imprest to carry the said turfe to the fortifications of this guarrison where needs requireth.[22]

Hauliers and workmen 'about the fortificacions of this guarrison' received £20, while £10 was reserved out of the money collected for the monthly pay of the garrison to buy spades, shovels and pickaxes for the work.[23] The speed with which the defences had returned to their ruinous state after the immediate crises of 1643–5 shows the strain that the city was under in trying to provide for its defence. These later works probably included the widening of the existing town ditches to match those dug around the bastions in 1643. A recent watching brief has suggested that the ditch beside the East Gate was widened to 12 m. The drawbridges were also repaired at a cost of £138 13s 8d.[24]

The garrison had also been raised back to its 1643 siege level of 1,400 men (after falling to only 600 in 1647). This was listed in September 1651 as comprising the governor, 1 master gunner, 2 gunners, 1 mate, 10 matroses (gunner's assistants), a storekeeper, 5 companies of foot from an army regiment (nominally 500 men), 640 private soldiers plus officers.[25]

In addition, Gloucester was expected to support the war elsewhere. In April 1651 the city had to provide 10 cavalrymen with 'backe, breast, pott, pistolls and sword' and 30 foot as a contribution to the force of 4,000 men to be sent to Ireland. This service was not popular. One of the foot, William Hooke, 'fled away from his quarters'.[26]

This period of crisis came to an end with Charles II's defeat at Worcester. Gloucester had sent ammunition, hay, hides, over seven hundred dozen loaves of bread and 'fourty barrels of stronge beere', together with a cask of special 'double beer' for Oliver Cromwell before the battle. On 11 October 1651 Cromwell was made High Steward of the city with an annuity of 100s p.a., and it was delivered with a present of the local delicacy of lampreys.

HALL AND PINNELL MAP OF THE DEFENCES

The periods 1644–5 and 1650–1 are therefore the context for the possible additions to the defences as shown on the Hall and Pinnell map of 1780 – compiled after the defences had been almost entirely levelled (and therefore not shown on the Kip Prospect of 1712). It shows an elaborate defence consisting of a double set of ditches with bastions at each angle, and an inner defence on the west side. It can be argued from the documentary evidence that some of these elements – such as a bastion on the south-east corner and at the East Gate – could not have been built by

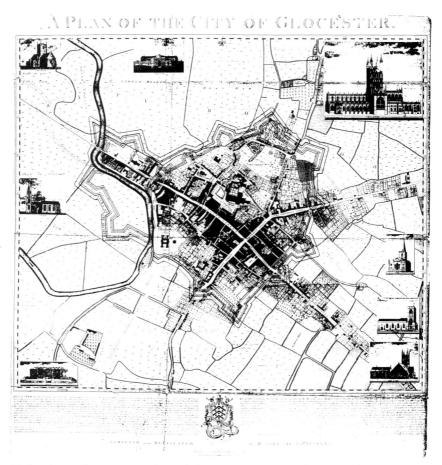

Hall and Pinnell map, 1780. This includes what is surmised to be a copy of a post-siege plan of intent to improve the defences. Only parts of this plan were completed. (*Copy of 1796 in Gloucestershire Records Office, with permission*)

August 1643. Neither does the plan show other (more temporary) parts of the defences – such as the internal retrenchment between the South and East Gates – that were certainly built during the siege. In some areas the plan shows little appreciation of the local topography – running over marsh and across streams through which it would have been impractical to try to dig. This plan has, therefore, been interpreted as being based on a now lost *plan of intent*, dating from 1644–51 but, in the event, only partially realized.

Evidence has been found for earthworks dug on the line of part of the Hall and Pinnell circuit outside the East Gate and on the south-east corner, which circumstantial evidence should date to the period 1644–51. Outside the East Gate, evidence was found in a salvage excavation of 1981 for an 8 m wide and 2.4 m deep 'v'-shaped ditch of similar profile to that of the South Gate bastion.[27] This was originally published as possibly being a breach of the city ditch adjacent to the East Gate, but the subsequent accumulation of evidence now means that it has been possible to reinterpret this as the ditch in front of the south face of a bastion.[28] The north face of this bastion was discovered in 1990 on a watching brief of a sewer trench along Clarence Street.[29] Both sightings match the locations recorded on the Hall and Pinnell map but the dating evidence is not precise enough to differentiate the years within the Civil War period. Observation of a British Telecom trench in 1982/4 and a sewer tunnel in 1990 outside the south-east angle of the city defences (in Brunswick Road at its junction with St Michael's Square) also produced evidence for the bottom of a ditch at a depth of 3.9 m–4.5 m below ground surface.[30] There was no direct dating evidence but the feature was on the line of the outer ditch as shown on the Hall and Pinnell map. Its former presence is still reflected in the name of Bastion House on Brunswick Road, and by a slight rise in land.

The Clarence Street sewer scheme (north of the East Gate) also provided evidence for a new seventeenth-century ditch running along the street, as an undefined feature over 3 m deep and containing seventeenth-century finds. This is the only place that a possible outer defence ditch, as recorded on the Hall and Pinnell map, has been discovered, but it clearly post-dates the descriptions by Dorney and Corbet of the defences there. The backfilled line of the ditch forms the basis of Clarence Street itself.

Some elements in the Hall and Pinnell map were clearly incomplete. It features an inner defence across Westgate Street, probably modelled on the one constructed during the siege in the south-east corner of the city. Some elements are obviously impractical (such as being bisected by a stream) but the intention appears to have been to extend the defence based on the 1643 'half moon' bastion at the 'Head of the Quay' (see p. 59). Outside the outer North Gate, two watching briefs suggested that an outer ditch to the bastion on the Hall and Pinnell model was begun on the south side (in the form of what was recovered as a 2 m deep ditch) but was not completed on the north side where no trace of a ditch was found.

DISMANTLING THE WAR EFFORT

The measures welcomed to protect the city in times of trouble were quickly resented when the immediate danger was over and the defeat of Charles II at Worcester in 1651 provided the final excuse to remove the garrison. On 1 January 1653 Parliament ordered the troops to be dispersed to field regiments. The brass cannon had also been removed and replaced with inferior iron ones, and weapons were collected to be sent to the Tower of London. The bastions (sconces) were also levelled in this year.[31] But this was not to be the end of the story.

There were further rumours of threats to the city in 1653–4 and in 1657–9, mostly arising from fears of conspiracies launched by the now-Royalist Massey. Although these never materialized they meant that Gloucester could not return completely to a peace footing. In 1654 Col. Wade readied 400 men for the defence of the city but fortunately the crisis passed.

A more serious threat came as the Protectorate entered its final phase and Charles II prepared to renew his claim to his kingdom. Massey was back in England in 1656, and a letter from Oliver Cromwell in December

Charges for dismantling the defences at the South Gate bastion. (*Gloucestershire Records Office, with permission*)

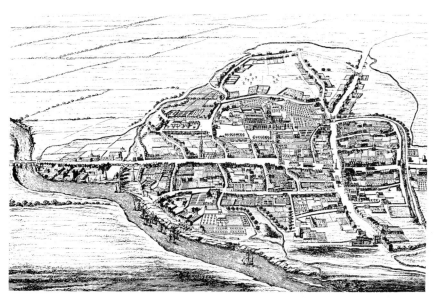

Most of the evidence for the defences had been destroyed before the time of the Kip map of 1712

1657 read 'they have a designe on your citie'.[32] In December of that year a Committee was established 'to view all the decays of the walls, gates and fences of this City', but there is no evidence that any extensive work was carried out on the defences as a result. A new garrison was, however, sent to Gloucester. In 1658 a reinforcement of a troop of horse arrived from London, and in November 1659 the mayor and aldermen complained to the Committee of Safety in London of the continued costs of quartering troops in public houses (which was also interfering with normal business), and paying for the costs of the watchfires and candles of the guards. These troops included three companies of Col. Cockrin's foot, and a troop of Col. Berrye's cavalry which had used up all of the hay in the city. Councillors had also been forced to take troops into their own houses. Unfortunately the Committee was little impressed by the city's excuses and sternly made it clear that these expenses were expected to be met.[33] Fortunately, the three companies of foot were moved to London in January but the continued problem of increasingly disorderly troops was probably the final straw in turning the city's loyalties back towards the monarchy.

Chaos now began to ensue. On 4 January 1660 there was a mutiny as officers of the garrison argued over whether to support Monck or Lambert as their two armies marched to what seemed to be another Civil War. Order collapsed as troops following Captain Coats to join Monck were attacked and their colours seized.[34] Troops then took arms from the magazine and caused an uproar in the streets.

In February James Stephens and William Cook, two aldermen, were arrested for their Royalist sympathies.[35] However, Massey returned openly to the city on 31 March to stand as an MP. Although he suffered an attack, he was duly elected, along with James Stephens (see Appendix 2, p. 176). Gloucester had, in effect, voted for the restoration of the monarchy. On 15 May, Charles II was proclaimed in the city and the conduits ran with wine. The days of Gloucester's championship of the parliamentary cause were now hastily put aside and referred to as 'clouds of error and infamy' in the loyal greeting sent by the Corporation on 25 June. They condemned the execution of Charles I and begged pardon. To further distance themselves from those heady days of August and September 1643 they now claimed that civil authority had been overruled by the military.[36]

SURVIVAL OF THE EVIDENCE

Much of the evidence for the Civil War defences therefore was removed in the 1650s, prior to the Restoration and the order to finally raze the defences. The sconces at East, South and North Gates, St Oswald's and Friar's Orchard were levelled in 1653 at a cost of £34 10s 10d.[37] The soil was used in the west part of town to raise flood-threatened areas.[38] Thus 'Paid Thomas Birke for ridding away the dirte att Southgate 0-3-0d'.[39] Over 1 m of seventeenth-century soil was found piled over the late medieval street surfaces and against the wall of St Nicholas's church on Lower Westgate Street. Finally, with the Restoration, the walls of Gloucester were ordered to be razed in 1662.

Nevertheless, the ditches probably survived as topographic features for a considerable period. That on the east side of the South Gate was being used as a rubbish dump until the very end of the seventeenth century, when Green Dragon Lane was finally re-established over the line of its slumped fill. The fills from the defence ditch fell into three broad horizons. The finds from the levels of initial silting in the Southgate Street ditch probably reflect assemblages of the 1640s and 1650s as the defences fell into disrepair and began to be used as rubbish tips. The assemblage of

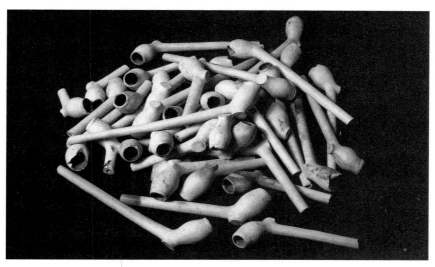

Clay tobacco pipes dating to the 1650s found in the lowest fill of the Civil War ditch excavated on Southgate Street in 1983. (*P. Greatorex for Gloucester City Museums*)

clay pipes from this silt is particularly notable in including a distinct group dating to the period up to 1650, with long stems indicating a fresh, undisturbed deposit.[40] This level of fill was succeeded by thick deposits that reflect the pushing back of the earth rampart during 1653. The latter contained high degrees of residual material deriving from the layers through which the ditch had originally been cut. However, the main bulk of the finds derived from later seventeenth-century rubbish dumped into the surviving hollow. Finally, the ditch on the east side of Southgate Street was surfaced in at the end of the seventeenth century by a series of metallings representing the re-establishment of Green Dragon Lane.

A large part of the south suburb was left abandoned and derelict for a considerable period after the siege and the city council tried to landscape the area in an early attempt to create a civic amenity (including walks down to the river in 1648).[41] On the west side of the street the surviving stone walls of the houses were robbed away and the site levelled. The rampart behind the defence ditch was flattened and the soil spread riverwards to the west. Over 2 m of seventeenth-century deposits were found pushed over the line of Small Lane (which had run parallel to Southgate Street and 40 m behind it). The ditch itself was made safe: 'Paid to Wm Terrett for rayling the trench at Southgate 8-10-0d'.[42] On the east side of the street, the ruins of the razed houses were also cleared, and in one excavated instance a cesspit was capped with clay to seal the noxious smells and so improve the environment.

The attempt to tidy up in the area was, however, thwarted by the establishment of a possible tannery or dyeing industry on the west side of Southgate Street. Excavation in 1989 revealed a number of emplacements for small tanks and large hearths, together with a series of drains, that may have been part of a series of dye houses. There is supporting documentary evidence from 1648 for the use of part of the adjacent site of St Owen to dry cloth.[43] The features respected the alignment of the former Civil War bastion, suggesting that the latter remained as a topographical feature for a considerable time, despite the King's order to raze them in 1660. It is possible that the road continued to be diverted around the side of the bastion for a period, as is also suggested by a documentary reference regarding the Alvin Gate.[44] The earthworks were evidently very difficult to eradicate as Lord Herbert himself complained in 1662 as he tried to make breaches in the wall and removed the 'flankers' (bastions).[45]

Seventeeth-century tannery on Southgate Street built beside the backfilled defences and showing the emplacements for the vats in which the hides were soaked. (*M. Atkin for Gloucester City Museums*)

CHAPTER 9

Effects of the Siege and the Civil War

POLITICAL CHANGE

Clarendon acknowledged that while King Charles was engaged at Gloucester he 'thereby gave respite to the distracted spirits at London, to breathe and compose themselves; and, more methodically than they had hoped to have done, to prepare for their preservation, and accomplishing their own ends; which att that time seemed almost desperate and incurable'.[1] Thus the most long-lasting effect of the siege of Gloucester is its claim to have diverted King Charles from marching on London and winning a decisive victory against Parliament, thereby changing the course of English history. The successful outcome to the siege was undoubtedly an important boost to parliamentary morale and brought a halt to the talk of peace.

Ultimately, though, the Royalists triumphed and, as they exacted their revenge on Gloucester, they altered its local political make-up. Before the Civil War and during the Interregnum much of the initiative had been in the hands of local merchants and traders. In a speech of 1652 Dorney concluded that one of the reasons for the deterioration of trade in the city was because 'the gentry were much cooled in their affections to this City, because it had so constantly adhered unto, and so faithfully acted for the Parliament . . .'.[2] The Restoration saw a new increase in the influence of the Royalist-biased gentry in the city's affairs. They were elected as MPs and it was they who acted as commissioners under the 1661 Corporation Act to purge the former parliamentarians from the city council. Notable names from the opponents of Gloucester during 1643 appear on the list of

Commissioners, including Lord Herbert and Sir John Wyntour. Three-quarters of the Corporation changed during 1662–3, with the dismissed including the former mayor, Dennis Wise, William Singleton and Luke Nourse who had all been officers of the Town regiment during the siege. Now men such as the Royalist Thomas Price took control. Other noted Parliamentarians such as Thomas Pury had already died (his son retreating into obscurity at Taynton). In part these changes may have saved the city from the further wrath of Charles II. After initially being removed from the city's control, Dudston and Kings Barton were restored to the city in 1662. However, such changes caused much resentment at the time and an underlying hostility to the new order remained for a considerable period.

One curious survivor of the purge was Toby Jordan, the bookseller who had delivered the city's defiant refusal to surrender in 1643. As mayor in 1659 he was implicated in Massey's abortive attempt to seize the city and in 1662 was appointed coroner by the same order that removed the other formal rebel aldermen from the council. Nicholas Webb and William Hodges, who had taken prominent roles during the proceedings, also temporarily retained their place as aldermen.

HUMAN COST

If today we see the Civil Wars as a rather picturesque episode of British history then we should remember that a minimum estimate of around eighty-five thousand men died during the fighting. Another hundred thousand or so may have died as an indirect result of the wars, such as from disease. An unknown number were maimed for life. One Royalist officer during the war commented 'we bury more toes and fingers than we do men'. A recent estimate has suggested that in some cases the loss for local communities was, in proportion to the population of the times, greater than in the First World War.[3] Most died in the scattered and small-scale skirmishes that were a feature of the war, and in actions such as the siege of Gloucester rather than the more famous set-piece battles.

The final death toll at the siege of Gloucester was widely disputed. The Royalists (in *Mercurius Aulicus*) claimed as few as a hundred but Parliamentary sources put it as high as fifteen hundred. The Royalists themselves did, however, admit that the toll of wounded and maimed was nine hundred, in other words those that had been taken off by boat to Bristol at the end of the siege. By contrast, the city claimed to have lost at

Part of the Royalist Welsh army was trapped at Barber's Bridge after fleeing from the skirmish at Highnam in March 1643. The monument is to those killed in the fighting, whose bodies were discovered here in the nineteenth century. The site of the bridge is *c.* 100 m north

most fifty. Most of these, according to Sergeant Foster in his *Perfect Diurnal,* were reportedly 'shot in the head in peeping through some holes at the enemy' – demonstrating an enthusiastic but ill-advised curiosity in the progress of proceedings.[4] But this comment takes no account of the dead reported by the Royalists in the trenches or killed in the assault on the Kingsholm battery. In essence, the city was refusing to admit that any significant number of troops were killed in the actual fighting. Thus when we compare the accounts of two days of the most intense fighting for which both sides give casualty figures, we find wildly varying conclusions (see p. 98). The first casualty of war is, indeed, truth!

Nevertheless, a low death toll on the city side can be confirmed by the absence of any increase in deaths recorded in the surviving parish registers. One local fatality is recorded as the son of John Richardson, and this was given as a reason for allowing his old and disabled father to become a free-man and so qualify for a place in an almshouse. But where were the Royalist dead buried? The only definitely-identified burial from a casualty of the siege is a gravestone in Hempsted churchyard to the Royalist, Captain John Freeman, who was 'pierced through by the stroke of a gun-ner's bullet at the siege of Gloucester'. There is also evidence for a war

In Hempsted churchyard there is a tomb to Captain John Freeman, a Royalist officer killed on 9 August. The Latin inscription reads: 'Here lieth John Freeman, Captain of horse, son of John Freeman, of Bushley, in the county of Worcester, Gentleman, pierced through by the stroke of a gunner's bullet at the siege of Gloucester, in the camp of the King'

grave around Barber's Bridge where some, at least, of the five hundred dead from the skirmish at Highnam in March 1643 are buried (see p. 29). Burials were first recorded nearby while cutting a canal in the 1790s. Eighty-six burials were recovered from beside Barber's Bridge in the nineteenth century and the site is marked by a monument erected soon after. Further burials were discovered during road-widening there in the 1970s. Local tradition in the late nineteenth century also identified pits near 'Whitehall' in Brookthorpe as being the graves of those killed during the skirmishes there immediately before the siege. There is, however, no other tradition of any similar war grave for the siege itself. Washbourn believed that some of the burials discovered in Kingsholm (part of an extensive Roman cemetery) were from the Civil War.[5] This is probably a reference to an earlier report from Kingsholm that 'workmen found a body in boots, spurs, and a buff coat with buttons'.[6] No supporting evidence for this has ever been found in the extensive programme of watching briefs subsequently carried out in the area. Three-quarters of St Margaret's Hospital on London Road was destroyed during an attack on Royalist quarters there on 14 August and a number of irregularly orientated, shallow graves have recently been found south of the chapel in 1990 which *may* date from the siege.[7]

What happened to the rest of the dead? Some at least were removed from the frontline during the course of the siege. On Monday 21 August 'they suffered us to fetch off three dead men'. Stories of the time told of the dead being carried away,[8] but does a battlefield cemetery remain to be uncovered? Indeed, it may have been earlier during the construction of the canal, docks or the new housing estates and no one recognized the significance (much of St Owen's graveyard was likewise destroyed without record in the construction of the Docks in the mid-nineteenth century). Unfortunately there is no reference to match that from Berkeley in 1644 which tells of the military funerals of two of the parliamentary soldiers killed at the siege there – buried 'souldier like with the drumme and two peals of shott'.[9]

The city does, however, contain other monuments to casualties of the Civil War who were killed elsewhere. Against the north wall of the Cathedral Lady Chapel was a monument to Major-General Lawrence Crawford of the Scottish army and a veteran of the continental wars in Sweden and Germany. A Presbyterian like Massey, he had taken a notable role in the siege of York in 1644, and it was claimed that Cromwell had taken advice from him at the battle of Marston Moor. He was killed at the siege of Hereford in 1645. The monument contained a justification of the parliamentary cause and was therefore defaced at the Restoration.[10]

> To Vindicate rights human and divine
> The Crown of Sweden, and Palsgrave of the Rhine;
> And both the british senates having serv'd,
> With honour gain'd, and faithfulness preserv'd,
> The publick interest pleading with his sword,
> He died before the walls of Hereford.

There is also a monument in the cathedral to William White, initially a lieutenant and then promoted to captain in Massey's regiment during the siege, and who was later appointed governor of Berkeley Castle. During the siege he is mentioned as one of the officers who led the initial sally out to Wotton on 6 August. He was killed at Raglan Castle in 1646. His monument has also been defaced but originally read:

> What man more valiant than he that lies
> Intombed here after his victories?
> Let such as his undaunted courage knew,
> Live to report and witness what is true.
> In famous Berkeley Castle he was known
> As governor, tho' aged but twenty one,
> Maintaining still the cause which much renown,
> Which he at first for right and just did own.
> His name and house since conquering William's days
> Is registered; his life's deserving praise:
> Till death at Ragland Castle, by a wound,
> Ended his days, that so he might be crown'd
>
> [An.1646]

Worn-out leather shoes of styles dating to around the 1620s found in the 1650s fill of the city defence ditch outside the South Gate (Southgate Gallery site). Their longevity provides some idea of the quality of the local product. (*M. Atkin for Gloucester City Museums*)

In the church of St John Northgate there is a monument to Thomas Price who was a Royalist officer, noted by Sir Edward Walker as one of the King's loyal subjects in the city, who fought elsewhere and was 'often wounded and once left for dead'. He died in 1679. He had been a member of the Common Council before the Civil War and quickly re-established himself in the city at the Restoration. He was sheriff in 1661 and then mayor in 1666.

SOCIAL CHANGE

The presence of the large and unruly garrison inevitably brought some social upheaval. There was a marked increase in cases involving 'tippling' and common selling of beer in 1641–5 as the local brewing industry tried to keep up with the demands of the garrison. Other consequences were more serious as law and order broke down. Corbet spoke of 'not a lawyer left in the country, no court of equity to relieve the oppressed. . . . No landlord could receive his rent, no intercourse of trade between man and man.'[11] The soldiers 'gave themselves up to spoile and rapine' and those within the city were 'mutinous and desperate'.[12]

There was a personal cost, too, after the battles were over and the troops found that their normal livelihood had been disrupted. A few lucky individuals (such as John Barnewood, hero of the grenade attack on the East Gate mine) managed to gain admission as freemen on account of their military service, but otherwise the Council found it necessary to provide funds to maintain sick and wounded soldiers through an Act of 7 April 1643.[13] In October 1643 and May 1644 Jasper Clutterbuck was being paid to look after the sick and wounded.[14] One of these was John Assard, 'a poor man' who 'did good service at the time of the siege and is now in misery', who was given 30s for his relief.[15] A woman, Jane Heard, was given £1 in October 1643 after having been wounded during the siege in Friar's Orchard. The effects were long-lasting. In 1657 the widow of Thomas Downe was paid a quarterly pension of 4s as her husband had also been wounded in Friar's Orchard.[16]

There was inevitable fraternizing between garrison and citizens. In November 1659 the city was complaining about 'the increase of our poore by many families, in regard to their marriages of souldiers during the former troubles; this city is much empoverished'.[17] Some of the liaisons may seem surprising. The daughter of Alderman Thomas Pury secretly married a Royalist held in Gloucester prison during a siege. William Leigh of Longborough, an ardent Royalist, had been High Sheriff of

Gloucestershire in 1634 and had aroused considerable animosity through his attempts to collect the Ship Money. (His mother was later accused of threatening to hang a servant for being unwilling to join the Royalist forces.) Both William and his estates were seized at the start of the Civil War, and while imprisoned in Gloucester he fell in love with Joanna Pury, then aged only nineteen years. William was thirty-nine years old. The thought that this was an attractive match to get him out of a predicament cannot have failed to pass through Leigh's mind. Certainly, Pury managed to arrange a pardon and restoration of Leigh's estates. It may be no coincidence that the Leighs were the first of the county gentry to recover sufficiently to contemplate rebuilding work at their house at Adlestrop, but, whatever the original reason for their match, they appear to have lived happily together until their deaths in 1689 and 1690 when Joanna was sixty-five and William was eighty-six.

The more unusual consequence of the Civil War was to split families. Highnam House, the property of Sir Robert Cooke, the noted parliamentary commander, was seized and pillaged by the Royalists in March 1643. However, Cooke's eldest son fought on the Royalist side and so the estate as a whole was then seized by Parliament.

REBUILDING THE CITY

Gloucester was quick to try to restore the physical damage to the fabric of the city. Only three months after the seige, repair-work began to Crypt school, using materials salvaged from St Owen's church.[18] Nevertheless, there were complaints of 'continual decay' in the city during the 1650s and the churches of St Mary de Grace (in the middle of the east end of Westgate Street) and St Aldate (now the site of Debenhams on The Oxbode) were demolished in 1652 and 1653 respectively, in order to provide materials to rebuild St Michael's at The Cross. Most of St Katherine's (the north aisle of the former St Oswald's priory) was also demolished in 1655. By 1648 the Bishop's Palace at Over, occupied by the Welsh army in August 1643, had been reduced to nothing 'but a few ruinous walls'.[19] During the First Civil War, Gloucester played down the destruction caused by the siege, although triumphing in the resolve that they had shown in burning down their suburbs. Dorney, in a speech of 5 October 1646, referred to the city after the burning of the suburbs as 'a garment without skirts, which we are willing to part withall, lest our enemies

St Nicholas's church, Westgate Street. The top of the spire was hit in the siege and, after the war, material was carted away from the defences and used to raise the level of Westgate Street in order to help protect against flooding

should sit upon them'.[20] However, in 1649–50 a fresh survey of the extent of destruction was ordered by the new mayor, James Stephens, which for the first time admitted significant damage within the city itself.[21] By 1651 the city council was asserting that the householders within the city walls were 'in much want and misery' and therefore requiring additional compensation.[22]

The suburbs had been almost completely destroyed. The 241 houses lost included 88 outside the South Gate in Lower Southgate Street, Small Lane and Severn Street; 67 houses had been destroyed in the east suburb on Barton Street; 69 houses in the north suburb in Newland, Fete Lane and Brook Street; and 17 houses in Kingsholm and beyond the Alvin Gate.[23] These areas were only slowly rebuilt. The Kip Prospect of 1712 shows a mere four houses outside the South Gate (where there had been over eighty). One aspect of considerable interest is to find evidence for where both the dispossessed and the enlarged garrison (totalling around

Part of the wooden gate for the South Gate of Gloucester, rebuilt in 1644. Now in the Folk Museum. (*P. Greatorex for Gloucester City Museums*)

two and a half to three thousand) were housed during the siege and its aftermath. Large parts of the suburbs were not rebuilt until the eighteenth century and it is likely that some, at least, of the dispossessed were housed in subdivided rentals for the short term. The final destruction of the suburbs may have had as much to do with the effects of their abandonment over the winters of 1643–5, during the continuing fear of fresh siege, than with the initial fires of August 1643. A 'siege mentality' clearly existed in the city for a considerable time that made people unwilling to resettle outside the security of the defences. As a result, the crisis occasioned a considerable permanent expansion of the better-quality housing stock into areas within the city walls that had been open land for over two centuries. The siege did, therefore, radically change the pattern of topographic development in the city. New houses were built on Bearland and Marybone Park – beside the ruins of the castle and the site of the medieval 'dunghills'. 'And now in stead of the old suburbs without this city (where there are traces of ruins) there is a new street building within the city.'[24] Bearland was renamed New Street following the new building work carried out between the quay and the west end of Longsmith Street after the siege. Eleven new plots were leased in Marybone Park in 1644, 1645 and 1647 for a row of buildings fronting Quay Street, the largest of these being the New Bear Inn on the junction of Castle Lane and Quay Street.[25] A number of the building leases went to those who had lost property in the suburbs.

Unfortunately, there is still little coherent archaeological evidence of domestic housing in the post-medieval period – being largely confined to observations in service trenches, rather than from large-scale structural evidence or stratified groups of material.[26]

Not all the damage had been occasioned by the siege of 1643 and parliamentary forces did their own damage. Col. Morgan, the governor in 1645, seems to have been justifiably reluctant to allow the Scots army of Alexander Leslie (Earl of Levan) to pass through the city in September of that year, on their way from Hereford to Warwick. His doubts were justified. They are generally believed to have been the culprits who smashed stained glass windows in the cathedral cloisters, while stabling their horses there.[27] The thirteenth-century effigy of Duke Robert of Normandy was also smashed at some point between 1654 and 1660, but was expertly

The now-peaceful cloisters of Gloucester Cathedral were turned into cavalry stables by the Scottish army that passed through the city in 1645. They are also likely to have caused damage to the stained glass windows at the same time

145

restored after the Restoration. The chapter property was sequestered in 1648 and some of the houses in the precinct were used to accommodate the Puritan preachers. There was said to have been a plot to demolish the cathedral and profit from the sale of materials, and part of the Little Cloister and the Lady Chapel began to be pulled down.[28] Fortunately others did appreciate the building – described by Dorney in 1652 as 'the great ornament of this city' – and the site was protected. It was granted to the mayor and burgesses in 1656. Thomas Pury the younger played a notable role in establishing the basis of the still-surviving cathedral library in 1648.

ECONOMIC COST

Gloucester certainly paid an economic cost for its role in the Civil War. The initial costs of building the defences and establishing the garrison have been referred to above (p. 36). The total cost of the garrison was estimated (in 1645) to have been £34,000.[29] Even during the siege the Corporation needed to find new ways to ensure that the troops were paid. On 29 August 1643 the Common Council ordered that every person obliged to contribute to the poor relief should pay a double assessment. The money so raised was to be distributed to those engaged on active service as well as to such others who were unfit for work.[30] If the citizens were not able to offer some promise of payment then past experience suggested that the troops may have deserted. A Royalist account claimed that the arrears owing to the garrison immediately after the siege amounted to £8,000.[31] The money promised from Parliament for this purpose did not materialize and in November 1643 the city was forced to pay part of the garrison's arrears from plate bought from Sir Robert Pye at 4s 4d per ounce. Three hundred pounds worth was given to Massey and the equivalent of one month's pay to the officers of the Town regiment 'assuring them of Parliament's intention, as soon as possibly they can, both to satisfy the engagement due to the cittye and to pay their fomer arrears'.[32] Plate was also used to buy muskets, match and powder. In May 1644 £1,530 was distributed to the officers of the garrison regiments, but this was still probably made out of local collections.[33] In August 1644, the city was faced with a weekly assessment of £100 to maintain the garrison.

The strain on the city finances and the effects of the war on the local economy are clearly seen in both the falling rent roll and the rise in rent arrears 1642–5.[34]

Table 3

Year	Rent Roll	Arrears	% Arrears
1640–1	£490 4s 4d	–	–
1641–2	£497 4s 8d	£27 0s 1d	5.0%
1642–3	£497 4s 8d	£172 9s 8d	34.5%
1643–4	£442 17s 0d	£189 6s 10d	42.8%
1644–5	£430 9s 5d	£149 12s 11d	34.8%
1645–6	£581 3s 4d	£108 4s 6½d	18.6%

There may, however, have been a more positive impact in that the siege and subsequent campaigns acted as a temporary spur to some local industries – a number of which were in dire straits before the war – with Gloucester becoming, by necessity, the main parliamentary supply centre for the region. Thus, carpenters and masons worked on the defences, blacksmiths made locks, chains and military hardware, coopers made the barrels for the gunpowder while some local craftsmen learnt new skills such as the bellfounders who made musket balls and grenadoes (see Appendix 3).

By 1646 a remarkable recovery had been made due partly to re-letting the land it had entered for non-payment and by paying off some of the loans forced on the Corporation in 1642–3. Parliament had also provided some additional assistance by awarding the city in March 1645 one-third of the profits from the import of currants in order to help maintain the garrison. They were also able to seize money from 'delinquent' Royalists. Thus, in March 1647, they took the £4,000 from Henry Poole that he owed to Sir Humphrey Tracey.

The Third Civil War renewed the strain of paying for building work and an enlarged garrison. In 1651 and 1654 there were complaints that six of the companies consisted of 'handicrafts men and other labourers and servauntes' who could not support themselves and therefore asked Parliament for additional support.[35] These men were also a significant part of the city workforce that Gloucester had clearly lost to other duties. The continuing strain of supporting a garrison right up to 1660 was undoubtedly a critical factor in eventually turning the city towards Royalist sympathies. As early as 1652 Dorney was blaming the continued presence of the garrison as a major reason for the decline of trade in the city. He commented 'when this City had lesse security, then it had more trading, and that if the Garrison might be removed from it, the ancient trade would return unto it.'[36] By the time of the Hearth Tax returns of the 1660s Gloucester had fallen to twenty-seventh in the list of provincial towns.[37]

While there was inevitably some temporary disruption of trade routes 1643–5, it is difficult to judge how important this was in the longer term. There is, for example, no evidence to suggest that new sources of pottery had to be found during the period or that it stimulated a more local production (the main change came in the 1680s with the development of the Newent pottery).[38] A great deal of the pottery came from sources in the Forest of Dean, but the potters there may have been able to avoid the worst excesses of the violence in the area by virtue of their already itinerant existence.

Similarly with the manufacture of clay pipes. Restrictions on production had been removed by the abolition of the London monopoly in 1640 and this had led to a major production centre being established at Bristol. The products of this would have been inaccessible to Gloucester for most of the war, but there is no valid evidence to suggest that a local industry took advantage of this. The local pipes of this period are unmarked and therefore it is difficult to be certain. The earliest recorded evidence of a pipemaker in Gloucester was from 1657 to 1666, during which time Thomas Cullemore, a pipemaker's apprentice from Bristol, moved here.[39]

Tobacco growing was one industry that certainly did prosper during the war years – by virtue of the fact that the warring sides were too embroiled to give it the attention it usually received. The crop had been grown in Gloucestershire, particularly around Winchcombe, from as early as 1619. It was declared illegal by Charles I because of its supposedly damaging effect on the export trade of the West Indies and America, and this led the growers to initially support Parliament in the conflict. The industry seems to have been left in peace until the end of the Second Civil War but then the tobacco growers soon found that they were equally under threat from Parliament – for the same reasons. The crop was prohibited in 1652, to be followed again by riots, but the order was delayed for a year in 1653 in return for the growers paying a levy of 3d on every pound of tobacco to help the Commonwealth coffers. In 1654 the people of Winchcombe raised 300 horse and foot to resist the troops sent down to destroy the crop and invited others to join them. This stand won another stay of execution.[40] Crops continued to be planted and in 1658 there was again armed resistance against parliamentary troops. A mere thirty-six cavalrymen sent to burn the crop were opposed by over two hundred of the local planters who refused to disperse. They were 'a rabble of men and women calling for blood for the tobacco, so that had there been any action, blood would have been split'.[41] The local militia and Justices of the Peace (many of whom were involved in the industry) gave only half-hearted support to the government. A letter to the secretary of the exiled Charles II claimed that the 'gates of Gloucester would be thrown open by Royalist sympathizers, sure of the ready support of 600 discontented tobacco planters in the neighbourhood'.[42] But this was merely wishful thinking.

By this time it is likely that the planters had grown cynical over offers of support and certainly the Restoration did nothing to help their cause. In 1667 troops had again to be sent to Winchcombe, 'a miserable poor place' according to Pepys, to again try to prevent the growing of the crop. Growing did, in fact, continue until the 1690s.

THE SURROUNDING COUNTRYSIDE

In many ways it was the country surrounding Gloucester that bore the main brunt of the effects of war as the armies moved to and fro. The experiences of John Chamberlayne, esquire, of Maugersbury (near Stow-on-the-Wold) were probably common as he suffered at the hands of both sides. In December 1642 he had to pay £25 to quarter 20 officers and 120 men of the Marquis of Hertford on their way to Oxford. Immediately after the siege of Gloucester in September 1643 he was forced to quarter troops from both sides. First part of the advancing Earl of Essex's relief army was billeted on him – and then part of the retreating Royalists! His accounts describe how: 'When my Ld of Essex His Army Mched to the reliefe of Glouc. they spent mee In Howse Hold Provision of Bread Bere cheese meate & provender . . . £6.' But later, 'Quartered upon the Breakinge up of Glouc: siedge 20ty men and Horses of the kings armye 3 dayes which come to . . . £4.'[43]

Not surprisingly, therefore, a recent study concludes that the Civil War brought the building work on the gentry's country houses to an almost complete stop.[44] Significantly, one of the first to recover was William Leigh's estate at Adlestrop Park in the 1650s; his marriage meant he was able to exploit both sides.

'. . . it is hardly to be credited, how many thousand sheep were in a few days destroyed'. Woodcut of 1642 depicting a soldier equipped with the profits of looting instead of his normal equipment

It was not a time to stand out from the crowd over one's principles. The well-known Royalist, Mr Rowland Bartlet of Castlemorton (in modern Hereford and Worcester, lying between Upton and Ledbury), suffered particularly badly. His house was sacked twice in September 1642 and three times within three days a year later. Finally, the men of the Earl of Essex's army 'rifled it of every thing that they could find, to the very kitchen stuff, which a soldier carried off in a small barrel upon his shoulder'.[45] Even neutrals could suffer through opportunism. The value of the Earl of Middlesex's Gloucestershire estates were halved between 1642 and 1647 by the non-payment of rents.

The besieging Royalist army was camped around Gloucester in a hostile neighbourhood but had to find food from somewhere. Some was provided by sympathetic gentry but plundering was rampant around the city. The Royalist Clarendon himself admitted

a very great license broke into the army both among officers and soldiers; the malignity of those parts being thought excuse for the exercise of any rapine or severity among the inhabitants. In so much

150

as it is hardly to be credited, how many thousand sheep were in a few days destroyed.[46]

One can imagine the dread of the local villagers when they saw the foraging parties heading their way. Animals were slaughtered, crops ruined, the menfolk pressed into service (as were the men of Barton Hundred and the Forest of Dean at the siege) or effectively held to ransom. Lord Herbert was wealthy enough to be the exception to these practices and took pride in paying for the costs of his army at the siege out of his own pocket. Lord Ruthven objected to this because it made the other Royalist commanders

Gloucestershire was ravaged by looters of both sides. Some houses were completely stripped of their possessions

appear more 'burdonsome' to the local population. Herbert retorted that the latter was a 'soldier of fortune, here today and God knows where tomorrow, and therefore needed not care for the love of the people'.[47]

Some destruction was more cold and calculating. Prince Rupert's devastating incursions into the Forest of Dean in 1645 were designed to cower the local population. But neither side was clear of guilt. Massey had also to deal with similar instances of looting by his own men in 1644 as they suffered from lack of pay. He was also accused by the Royalist news-books of doing £10,000 worth of damage in Gloucestershire and Herefordshire in May 1644, after he had unsuccessfully tried to take 'White Cross'.

In these circumstances it is not surprising that some in the Forest of Dean considered turning to banditry, and there was a general breakdown of law and order. Dorney complained in early 1643 that the sheriffs 'have not had the power of their county, nor yet of their goal: such is the condition of these times'.[48] Some villages such as Padsworth (see above) were at least temporarily deserted.

As in almost any war, stories of atrocities abounded on both sides, quickly fuelled by contemporary newsbooks. The Royalist *Mercurius Rusticus* tells of the plunder of Sudeley Castle in January 1643, and the desecration of the church and tombs by the troops from Gloucester, 'the lower part of it they make their stable, the chancel their slaughter-house'.[49] Around the same time, the parson of Minchinhampton was allegedly savagely beaten and robbed by Captain Jeremy Buck and his men for the excuse that 'he read the common-prayers at length, and that he had published the kings proclamation with a loud voice'. More prosaically, he had also supplied a musket, armour and horse for the Royalists.[50]

CHAPTER 10

Conclusion

And it must be confessed, that governor gave a stop to the career of the King's good success, and from his pertinacious defence of that place, the Parliament had time to recover their broken forces, and more broken spirits; and may acknowledge to this rise the greatness to which they afterwards aspired.[1]

Thus was the assessment of Clarendon on the siege of Gloucester. The importance of this period in Gloucester's history cannot be under-estimated, either in terms of the way in which Gloucester's resistance dur-ing the siege helped shape the course of national events, or the changes in the topographic development of the city.

Little direct artefactual evidence for the siege has survived. A number of Civil War period helmets were found at the scene of the skirmish at Brookthorpe.[2] A further helmet was found at Quedgeley, there is scrap from a possible ammunition forge from Longlevens, a few musket balls from Southgate Street and Kingsholm, a cannon ball from a culverin from outside the East Gate and, most notably, a rare example of a simple wooden priming flask from one of the ditch sections excavated on Southgate Street. The paucity of artefacts is an important reminder of the limitations of archaeological sources in defining individual historic events. Apart from such military items, most other finds of the general period are not capable of being dated to the precision of a single year or even decade. And yet Gloucester was the site of a major battle involving over thirty-one thou-sand men. Where is the rest of the material that was worn by the soldiers or the large number of iron cannon balls that were hurled to and from the city's walls? Most of the evidence was carried away with the soldiers. Of items of equipment that they may have lost or thrown away, much was made of perishable materials – wood or leather that has rotted away. As for the ironwork, it was too valuable to simply discard and would have been melted down again for reuse.

153

Lead musket balls found on the Southgate Street excavations. One has been flattened by impact against a wall. Also shown are stones from St Owen's church, part-demolished prior to the siege. (*M. Atkin for Gloucester City Museums*)

The people of the city showed great resolve and unity under pressure. In part, this has been undervalued due to the attention paid to Massey as an individual. While undoubtedly the driving force behind the campaigns, he relied both on the willingness of the people to accept privation and also the enterprise of his field officers in the sallies.

With hindsight it is possible to argue that Charles I sealed his own fate by rejecting the tactic of immediate assault in order to spare his subjects. But how close did the city actually come to defeat – and would the assault on the East Gate have succeeded in just a few more days if Essex had not arrived in time? The worries of those last days in August and early September are clearly reflected in the hurried construction of secondary lines of defence. The city was clearly preparing, tremulously, for the main defences to fall. The ferocity of the sallies attributed to Massey on 29 August and 2/3 September may be a mark of the sense of urgency and desperation at that time. Those fears of a breakthrough are also visible in the attention given to inner defences on the proposed improvements to the defences as shown on the Hall and Pinnell map.

What would have happened if the city had fallen? Contemporaries were agreed that the time taken up at Gloucester was an important factor in King Charles ultimately losing the war. How might national history have been differently shaped if he had won? What sort of parliament might we have? Dorney reported how Judge Wilde referred to the people of Gloucester as 'the conservators of the parliament of England'.[3] This is the stuff of the great, unanswerable, 'ifs' and 'buts' of history!

Of more immediate concern to the beleaguered inhabitants – what would have happened to the people of Gloucester had the Royalist armies entered the city in 1643? Would the scenes have been as Lucy Hutchinson described as Nottingham fell, when 'the brave men turn cowards, fear unnerves the most mighty, makes the generous base, and great men do those things that they blush to think on'.[4]

In 1643 Gloucester appeared to stand alone with the future of the parliamentary side resting on its survival. Yet seventeen years later the city was preparing to welcome Charles II with open arms. Even stranger, it was doing so with the help of its hero of 1643, Edward Massey – now a hero to the Royalists. However, the mood of the country in 1660 was very different to those strident days of 1643. Another irony was that in February 1660, with echoes back to one of the original causes of the Civil War, a proclamation of lords, knights and gentlemen of Gloucestershire (i.e. those original opponents of Parliament in the county) protested against all assemblies that imposed taxes without the consent of Parliament (as a criticism of the Rump Parliament, deemed unconstitutional).

With the Restoration of Charles II, those days of pride in 1643 became an embarrassment, not concealed by the Corporation trying to blame the military for overruling civilian government. The exhortation to 'Ever remember the fifth of September' was removed in 1670 and was then politely forgotten. It seems likely that some effort was also made to doctor the official records of the time. It is certainly true that the Council Minutes contain little information as to the events of the Civil War, a fact which cannot wholly be explained by the separate responsibilities of the Committee for Defence. In a Minute of 2 August 1672

This house doth agree that mr Maior and two or three of the Aldermen of this City do peruse all and singular the Acts of Common Council of this City made in the time of the late troubles

155

Statue of Charles II erected after the Restoration (by Stephen Baldwin), originally at the Wheat Market on Southgate Street but now in St Mary's Square

tending to schisme or rebellion and to make a report to this house of all such Acts that they think fit to be expunged and defaced.[5]

We are now able to look back on this exciting period in Gloucester's history in a more detached fashion. A great deal remains to be learned but the opportunities are receding. Much of the land across which the defences and siegeworks were constructed has been developed and opportunities for further excavation are therefore restricted. In the mean time, it will be clear how far the work of excavation, watching briefs and documentary research has acted in partnership to enable this survey of evidence to be completed.

The City Arms that were granted in 1653 record the heroism of the siege in the form of a lion within a ring of defences and holding both a trowel and sword to commemorate the efforts of the builders of the defences and the garrison. It is hoped that this book has also shown how the trowel can still be put to good use to uncover this dramatic era in Gloucester's history.

The present Coat of Arms for Gloucester is based on one granted in 1653. The lion holding a sword and trowel, rising out of a battlemented crown is a reminder, to this day, of the valiant defence of the city during 1643

A Civil War Tour of Gloucester

For such a dramatic period in Gloucester's history there seems little at first glance for the visitor to see. However, perseverance will be rewarded!

NORTHGATE STREET

Memorial to Thomas Price, St John Northgate. Thomas Price was a Royalist officer, wounded in action, who later became mayor of Gloucester.

WESTGATE STREET

The Cross. Massey kept his Main Guard here during the siege as a rapid response force in case of attack.

St Mary de Grace. Site of former church at the east end of the centre of Westgate Street. It was demolished after the war.

26 Westgate Street. Formerly reputed to be the headquarters of Massey, but a fine building that was in existence at the time of the siege none the less.

30 Westgate Street. One of the finest seventeenth-century houses in Gloucester. Mr Commeline's house at the time of the siege. It was hit by an incendiary shot during the night of Friday 25 August.

Old Crowne Inn. On Thursday 24 August a 20 lb cannon ball flew through the bedroom window and landed on a pillow.

St Nicholas's church. Top of spire (although not the present one) was shot off.

Folk Museum. A sixteenth-century building now containing a display of Civil War armour found in the district around Gloucester.

EASTGATE STREET

The East Gate. Preserved under Boots the Chemist. The East Gate was one of the main foci of the siege. It was bombarded with cannon and miners attempted to undermine it. The now-blocked sally port where John Barnewood led a raiding party to attack one of the mines is still visible.

SOUTHGATE STREET

St Mary de Crypt. Used as an ammunition magazine during the siege. The sundial on the south buttress of the chancel reputedly marks the spot where a cannon ball hit the church. Inside (on the north side of the chancel) is a gravestone to Thomas Pury, one of the principal leaders during the Civil War.
Greyfriars, off Southgate Street. Medieval friary used as Massey's quarters and a command post for a time during the siege. It was hit by cannon fire.

BRUNSWICK ROAD

Brunswick Road/Parliament Street. An interesting survival of the line of Gloucester's defences, preserved in the street pattern. The streets are built over the infilled defence ditch. Note Bastion House on Brunswick Road, opposite St Michael's Square, reflecting the location of a 1644–51 bastion.
Gaudy Green. Site of one of the main Royalist artillery batteries, directing fire against the south-east corner of the defences.

NORTH-WEST GLOUCESTER

Statue of Charles II, St Mary's Square. The statue was originally on the corner of the Wheat Market on Southgate Street.
St Mary de Lode, St Mary's Square. Used as prison for Royalists captured at Highnam, March 1643.
St Oswald's Priory. The priory was converted to use as St Katherine's parish church at the time of the sixteenth-century dissolution of the monasteries. It was demolished at the siege.

OUTER GLOUCESTER

Llanthony Priory, Llanthony Road. The tower of the church was demolished before the siege to prevent it being used by artillery spotters. The surviving monastic buildings would have formed part of the main Royalist camp at the siege.

Hempsted church, Hempsted. Tomb to Captain Freeman, killed during the siege.

Over Earthwork (adjacent to Over Hospital). Former Bishop's Palace converted into a sconce at time of the siege. Scene of Welsh débâcle when they tried to assault a deserted emplacement. The scale of the earthworks give a good impression of what the defences around Gloucester would have looked like. NOTE: This is a Scheduled Ancient Monument lying on private land. It is visible from the A40.

Highnam Earthwork, Highnam church. The present church is built on the site of the Civil War earthworks which were built alongside the road facing the Over Earthwork and the city.

Scriven's Conduit, Hillfield Gardens, London Road. Part of the city's water supply system at the time of the siege, cut off by the Royalists. It was originally sited in Southgate Street.

Lady Well and Well Cross, Robinswood Hill. Two medieval spring heads that were cut by the Royalists to interrupt the city water supply.

Select Bibliography

This covers only the most accessible sources which the general reader might find useful. Further details to the sources of original contemporary material are found in the notes to each chapter.

LOCAL

Fosbrooke, T.D., *An Original History of the City of Gloucester*. Gloucester, 1819 (reprinted 1986)

Heighway, C.M. , *Gloucester: a history and guide*. Gloucester, 1985

Washbourn, J., *Bibliotheca Gloucestrensis*. Gloucester, 1825

Whiting, J.S., *Gloucester Besieged*. Gloucester, 1975

GENERAL

Ashley, M., *The English Civil War*. Revised edn. Gloucester, 1990

Downing, T. and Millman, M., *Civil War*. London, 1991

Gardiner, S.R., *History of the Great Civil War 1642-1649*. London, 1893 (reprinted in 4 vols, 1987)

Manning, B., *The English People and the English Revolution 1640–1649*. London, 2nd edn, 1976

Morrill, J. (ed.), *The Impact of the English Civil War*. London, 1991

Roberts, K., *Soldiers of the English Civil War (1): Infantry*. London, 1989

Stone, L., *The Causes of the English Revolution 1529–1642*. London, 1973

Tincey, J., *Soldiers of the English Civil War (2): Cavalry*. London, 1990

OTHER

Partizan Press (Leigh-on-Sea, Essex) publish the regular *English Civil War Notes and Queries*

For those interested in re-enactments of the period there are two societies, both of which have Royalist and parliamentary 'armies':

English Civil War Society: c/o Thornton House, Bowridge Hill, Gillingham, Dorset SP8 5Qs

The Sealed Knot: 3 Fairview Rise, Crich, Matlock, Derbyshire, DE4 5DA.

Chronology

THE BACKGROUND TO THE CIVIL WARS

The causes of the eventual war were long-drawn and complex. They included political and economic resentment against the King for his imposition of taxes without parliamentary consent and fears as to the effect that the Catholic sympathies of himself and his French wife might have on the Protestant religion. The individual grievances were brought to crisis point by the wars against Scotland in 1639 and 1640 which forced the King to recall Parliament and confront his opponents. The Root and Branch petition against the Episcopacy and the impeachment of the King's friend Strafford and Archbishop Laud in 1640 saw Parliament test its strength. In 1641 Strafford was executed, the prerogative courts of Star Chamber and High Commission were abolished and the hated Ship Money tax was declared illegal. Parliament saw further opportunity in the Irish rebellion of October 1641 – the King needed an army but Parliament's condition was the demeaning 'Grand Remonstrance' which listed its grievances against the King.

Thus the scene was set for a war that had become almost inevitable.

THE FIRST CIVIL WAR

1642

4 Jan.	King tries to arrest the five leading dissident MPs in Parliament
23 April	King leaves London but is denied entry to Hull. This was the first act of outright rebellion
	King refuses to give up control of the Militia
May	Failure to agree a compromise settlement
22 Aug.	King raises standard at Nottingham. The war formally begins
23 Oct.	Battle of Edgehill – technical Royalist victory
12 Nov.	Battle at Turnham Green unites London against the King
	King establishes headquarters at Oxford

1643

24 March	Skirmish at Highnam – parliamentary victory
22 April	Siege of Lichfield – falls to Royalists

30 June	Battle of Adwalton Moor – Royalist victory
13 July	Battle of Roundway Down – Royalist victory
26 July	Siege of Bristol – falls to Royalists
10 Aug.	Siege of Gloucester – parliamentary victory on 5 September
20 Sept.	First Battle of Newbury – parliamentary victory
25 Sept.	'Solemn League and Covenant' allies Scots with King

1644
19 Jan.	Scots army enters England
20 April	Siege of York – eventually relieved by Royalists
2 July	Battle of Marston Moor – parliamentary victory
	York taken by Parliament
2 Sept.	Battle of Lostwithiel – Royalist victory
22 Oct.	Second Battle of Newbury – inconclusive

1645
10 Jan.	Execution of Archbishop Laud
3 April	'Self-Denying ordinance' prevents MPs (including Gloucester's former governor, Col. Massey) from also holding military posts
	Establishment of New Model Army
30 May	Siege of Leicester – taken by Royalists
14 June	Battle of Naseby – parliamentary victory
10 July	Battle of Langport – parliamentary victory
10 Sept.	Second Siege of Bristol – taken by Parliament
13 Sept.	Battle of Philiphaugh – Covenanter victory (supporting Parliament)
24 Sept.	Battle of Rowton Heath – parliamentary victory

1646
2 March	Prince of Wales leaves England
21 March	Last Royalist field army (under Lord Astley) surrenders at battle of Stow-on-the-Wold in Gloucestershire
	King Charles surrenders to Scots (who turn him over to Parliament)
8 May	Newark falls
25 June	Oxford falls

1647
18 Feb.	Parliament tries to disband New Model Army
	Army seizes King
16 June	Charges brought against eleven MPs who had criticized the army
11 Nov.	King escapes to Isle of Wight but is recaptured
26 Dec.	King makes new alliance with Scots and the angered Parliament breaks off peace negotiations

SECOND CIVIL WAR

1648

23 March	South Wales Rising
May	Kent Rising. Battle of Maidstone
27 Aug.	Essex Rising. Siege of Colchester – taken by Parliament
	Capture of Pontefract and Scarborough Castles by Royalists
11 July	Pembroke surrenders to Parliament
2 Aug.	Battle of Preston
6 Dec.	'Pride's Purge' of Parliament to remove peace party
	(Rump Parliament)

1649

30 Jan.	King Charles executed
5 Feb.	Scottish Covenanters proclaim Charles II
19 March	House of Lords abolished
19 May	Establishment of the Commonwealth
1 May	Army mutinies
15 Aug.	Cromwell's campaigns in Ireland

THIRD CIVIL WAR

1650

1 May	Treaty of Breda allies Charles II with Scots
26 June	Cromwell made Lord-General in place of Fairfax
3 Sept.	Battle of Dunbar – parliamentary victory

1651

1 Jan.	Charles II crowned at Scone
20 July	Battle of Inverkeithing – parliamentary victory
3 Sept.	Battle of Worcester – parliamentary victory
16 Oct.	Charles II flees

LATER EVENTS

1652	Start of Dutch War
	Settlement of Ireland
1653	Barebones Parliament
	Cromwell made Lord Protector
1654	End of Dutch War
1655	Penruddock's Rising
	Start of war with Spain

1656 Rule of Major-Generals
     Protectorate Parliament
1657 Cromwell refuses the crown
1658 Dissolution of Parliament
     End of war with Spain
     Death of Cromwell
     Succeeded by son Richard
1659 Richard Cromwell resigns
     Recall of Rump Parliament
     Act of Pardon and Indemnity
     Booth's Rising in Cheshire
     Monck marches from Scotland
1660 Monck enters London
     Parliamentary elections
     Declaration of Breda
     Covention Parliament
     Charles II restored

At 'Padsworth' Waller drew up his men 'in battalia' to decimate the advancing Royalist troops by volley fire

DIARY OF THE SIEGE OF GLOUCESTER, AUGUST–SEPTEMBER 1643

The town clerk of Gloucester, John Dorney, produced a day-by-day diary of the siege which can be expanded from other contemporary sources to give a flavour of the way in which the battle progressed. Because most of the sources are from parliamentary accounts, the narrative could be thought to give too much prominence to the city's attempts to disrupt the planning of the siege by its frequent sallies. These were of key importance to the campaign, but note also the move and counter-move of the battery of the walls and the city's efforts to improve the defences on those points, together with the mine and countermine. It is a ballet of war as the combatants gingerly move around one another, testing each other's strengths and weaknesses. What does not come over in the record of events is the equally important aspect of the siege of simply waiting – the long periods of inaction in which the city was meant to believe that it had no option but to surrender or be starved out or eventually stormed.

COUNTDOWN TO THE SIEGE

Saturday 5 Aug.	Royalist advance parties within 10 miles (16 km) of city.
Sunday 6 Aug.	Royalist camp established on Tredworth Field. Captain Blunt leads raiding party and takes 10 Royalists prisoner at Wotton.
Monday 7 Aug.	Royalists plunder Tuffley and then retreat to Brookthorpe where there was a skirmish.
Tuesday 8 Aug.	King's army reaches Berkeley.
Wednesday 9 Aug.	Skirmish at Barnwood.

THE SIEGE

Thursday 10 Aug.	King Charles arrives at Tredworth Field and commands the City to surrender – which it refuses to do.
	The city burns the suburbs.
	Royalists start digging trenches overnight and cut off water supply from Robinswood Hill.
Friday 11 Aug.	Welsh take the undefended Vineyard at Over.
	Lord General Ruthven establishes camp at Llanthony.
	Harcus leads raiding party from the South Gate.
Saturday 12 Aug.	Harcus leads further assault from Rignall Stile. Captain Gray attacks the Royalist quarters at Kingsholm. City burns down more houses in the suburbs.
	Royalists plant cannon outside the East Gate, make a redoubt in a field near Llanthony and prepare a battery in Gaudy Green.
	City lines city walls from South to East Gates with earth in response.
Sunday 13 Aug.	Welsh start to build bridge of '20 flat boats' in order to cross the River Severn and link their camp with that of the Worcester forces at Longford and Kingsholm.

	Artillery battery of city from Gaudy Green.
	City begins blocking up the South Gate.
Monday 14 Aug.	Captain Mallery leads raid to destroy cannon rumoured to now be at Kingsholm.
	He fails to find them but raids Royalist quarters at St Margaret's hospital and burns it down.
	Royalists make a mine near Rignall Stile.
Tuesday 15 Aug.	Grenades thrown into Royalist trenches, narrowly missing Prince Rupert.
Wednesday 16 Aug.	Royalists entrench between Barton Street and Friar's Barn.
	City lines houses adjoining the North Gate with earth.
	Captain Crispe leads raid out of North Gate which then turns to attack Friars Orchard trenches from behind. Reputedly kill over 100 Royalists.
	Royalists claim the death of 24 'blue coats' in a sally on the camp at Llanthony.
Thursday 17 Aug.	Royalists bring faggots during the night to try to cross the ditch by Friars Orchard but are driven back by musket fire from the walls.
Friday 18 Aug.	Welsh and Worcester forces unite at Kingsholm. One of the cannon from the Kingsholm battery brought up to the Awngate and adjoining sconces.
	Major Pudsey and Captain Gray lead large raid of over 400 men out from the North Gate to try to spike the Kingsholm cannon.
Saturday 19 Aug.	'Furious battery' on the south-east corner from the Gaudy Green and Rignall Stile batteries.
	In case that corner fell, the city began a breastwork running from the south side of Friar's Orchard to the East Gate.
	An attempt to cross the ditch is beaten off.
Sunday 20 Aug.	City kill two Royalist cannoneers.
Monday 21 Aug.	City attempt ambitious pincer movement to attack the Royalist trenches on the south and east sides of the city. Captain Stephenson leads 200 men (140 foot and 40 horse according to Royalist accounts) from the North Gate, aiming for the East Gate (but, by a misdirection, end up at Barton) while Captain Blunt takes a party by boat along River Severn and storm up Severn Street.
Wednesday 23 Aug.	City mounts further attacks from North Gate. Royalists receive supplies from Bristol.
	City lines Friar's Barn at the north-east corner of the defences on outside with earth.
Thursday 24 Aug.	Royalists make further appeal for city to surrender (by Bell and Hill).

	It rained that night (only rain of the siege).
Friday 25 Aug.	Further sally from the North Gate. Royalists fire burning shot from Gaudy Green in attempt to set light to buildings. The city fear that rumours may circulate to the effect that the city has fallen and therefore light fires from College Tower.
	Royalist Colonel Gerrard tries to fake the arrival of a relief army in order to draw the garrison out of its defences.
Saturday 26 Aug.	Renewed attempts to cross ditch on SE corner. Built a gallery.
	Royalists fire haystacks at Walham (which the city were still collecting in!).
	Earl of Essex leaves London with a relieving force of 8,000 men.
Monday 28 Aug.	City realizes Royalists trying to undermine East Gate and begin countermine.
Tuesday 29 Aug.	City begins to undermine wall on east side of Friar's Orchard to allow them to insert a cannon to batter the flanks of the Royalist trench.
Wednesday 30 Aug.	City begin to turn out cattle to graze in Little Meadow.
Friday 1 Sept.	City break into Royalist mine at East Gate.
Saturday 2 Sept.	Welsh advance to a ditch in Town Ham and fire on women and workmen collecting turves.
Sunday 3 Sept.	Assault planned on East Gate. City lines house over gate with earth and makes a strong breastwork there.
	Royalist message threatens no quarter.
Monday 4 Sept.	Royalist sick loaded on to boats for Bristol.
	Cavalry withdraw from around town.
	Relief is on its way.
Tuesday 5 Sept.	Royalists withdraw.

APPENDIX 2

Personalities of the Siege

1) CAPTAIN-LIEUTENANT HARCUS

One of the heroes of the siege was Captain-Lieutenant James Harcus. He was an officer in Massey's regiment (that of the Earl of Stamford) and was one of the military signatories of the refusal to surrender to the King on 10 August. He first appears in the accounts of the siege on 7 August when he took part in a raid out of the North Gate to Wotton, seizing ten prisoners. On Friday 11 August Harcus led a midnight raiding party out of the South Gate, 'beat the enemy from their trenches, and brought away many of their shovels and pickaxes'.[1]

The next morning he was in action again. He led a party out of the gate by Rignall Stile (making a bridge of ladders over the city ditch) and 'fell into the enemies trenches in Gaudy green, beat them out, gained some working tooles, arms, and prisoners, and retreated without losse of any, onely two wounded. This was a hot skirmish for the space of halfe an houre.'[2]

His end seems in character. On 15 August he was killed in the Friar's Orchard 'too venterously looking what execution a granado had done, which he then threw into the enemies trenches'.[3] This was presumably a hand-grenade – usually made of iron, pottery or even glass.

2) HENRY, LORD SPENCER

One of the King's officers and advisers was Henry, Lord Spencer. He described himself as 'General of Artillery' at the siege,[4] but otherwise nothing is known of his direct involvement apart from a reference to him counting the ordnance and arranging the import of arms and ammunition from Dunkirk.[5] He had also seen service in the 'Show Troop' of the King's cavalry at Edgehill and the siege of Bristol.

What makes him of especial interest is the survival of two of his letters home to his wife Dorothy, who was expecting their child at the time. The letters, originally published by Fosbrooke in 1819 are a fascinating mix of high politics, as he describes advice to the King and discussions with Dr Chillingworth and Lord Falkland, homely matters as he coyly describes a boil on his bottom and an appreciation of the horrors of civil war. He speaks of his periods in the trenches and the sounds of battle. We should also contrast his account of his stay as an officer in one of the 'little private cottages' with that of Welsh Thomas and his more lowly comrades living 'very hardy under the hedges' beside Llanthony Priory.

Henry Spencer, Earl of
Sunderland (*c.* 1619–43). An
engraving of an oil painting in
the collection of the Earl of
Spencer

His first letter from Gloucester was written as the armies gathered on 9 August. It is an important indication of the strains within the Royalist forces.

MY DEAREST HEART,
The King's sudden resolution of going before Gloucester hath extremely disappointed me; for when I went from Bristol on Monday morning he was resolved to come hither this day, and to that purpose sent his troop before. Upon this, I, and two or three gentlemen, agreed to meet his Majesty here this day, and to take the Bath in our way, which we did accordingly; by which means we missed his Majesty, being gone this morning towards Gloucester; and tomorrow morning he will be before it, where I intend to wait upon him. The King's going to Gloucester is in the opinion of most very unadvised. I find the Queen is unsatisfied with it; so is all the people of quality. I am not able to give you any account upon what grounds the King took this resolution.
August 9th, at sunset, 1643

Despite his doubts, Henry took his part within the siege with the second letter coming towards the end of the battle, introducing a rare glimpse of the humanity of the events. Here he talks of the tedium of life in the trenches and the progress of the mines. He refers to Massey's disruptive tactics of causing alarms but also refers to city casualties from a previous sally. One of his dinner companions was Dr Chillingworth of whom he does not seem to have too high an opinion.

171

MY DEAREST HEART,

Just as I was coming out of the trenches on Wednesday I received your letter of the 20th of this instant, which gave me so much satisfaction that it put all the inconveniences of this Siege out of my thoughts. At that instant, if I had followed my own inclinations, I had returned an answer to yours; writing to you and hearing from you being the most pleasant entertainment that I am capable of in any place; but especially here, where, but when I am in the trenches (which place is seldom without my company) I am more solitary than ever I was in my life; this country being full of little private cottages, in one of which I am quartered, where my Lord Falkland did me the honour last night to sup. Mr Chillingworth is now here with me in Sir Nicholas Selwin's place, who has been this week at Oxford; our little engineer comes not hither so much out of kindness to me as for his own conveniency, my quarter being three or four miles nearer the leaguer than my Lord of Devonshire's, with whom he stayed till he was commanded to make ready his engines with all possible speed. It is not to be imagined with what diligence and satisfaction (I mean to himself) he executes this command; for my part, I think it not unwisely done of him to change his profession, and I think you would have been of my mind if you had heard him dispute last night with my Lord Falkland in favour of Socinianism; wherein he was by his Lordship so often confounded that really it appears he has much more reason for his engine than his opinion. I put off my writing till last night, out of hopes that some thing here would have happened worthy of your knowledge more than what I wrote to you the day before; and you see what good company made me defer it last night, at which time I thought to have gone this morning; but I have got such an angry pimple, or rather a kind of small bile, in such a place, that as I cannot ride without pain, so I cannot with modesty make a more particular description. . . . find that we had only an alarm, which they gave to hinder our working, not daring to sally any more, being so well beaten the last time; the night before they offered to make a sally, forty or fifty of them being without their sally port, but we instantly beat them back. Our gallery will be finished within this day or two, and then we shall soon dispatch our mine, and them with it. Many of the soldiers are confident that we shall have the town within this four days, which I extremely long for, not that I am weary of the siege; for really, though we suffer many inconveniences, yet I am not ill pleased at this variety, so directly opposite to one another, as the being in the trenches with so much good company, together with the noise and tinta-marre of guns and drums, the horrid spectacles and hideous cries of dead and hurt men, is to the solitariness of my quarter. . . .

August 25th, from before Gloucester

Henry and Lord Falkland were both killed soon after the siege of Gloucester at the battle of Newbury in September 1643. His son was born two weeks later. Clarendon described him as 'a lord of great fortune, tender years (not being above three and twenty years of age), and an early judgement'.

3) LIEUTENANT-COLONEL EDWARD MASSEY — GOVERNOR OF GLOUCESTER

'incomparable conduct and courage'

Parliament

'A wonderful, vain and weak man but very busy and undertaking'

Clarendon

Edward Massey became the popular hero of the siege. At the time he was aged twenty-three, the son of a Cheshire gentleman from Coddington. There are a number of portraits and a written description (as part of a 'wanted' notice) in 1652 as being of 'brown hair, a middle stature, sanguine complexion'.

He did not come into the war as an idealist. Massey was a professional soldier and experienced military engineer who had seen many years' service in the continental wars. He had also been an engineer officer in Charles I's army on campaign in Scotland 1639-40. But his initial choice of allegiance in the war owed more to his perception of career prospects than to loyalty or belief. At the start of the Civil War he had tried to get a commission in the King's army at York, but having thought that there would not be sufficient chances of promotion there he first went to London ('where there was more money, and fewer officers'

Colonel Edward Massey, Governor of Gloucester during the siege of 1643. Oil painting by an unknown artist. (*Gloucester City Museum collection*)

according to Clarendon), and eventually joined the parliamentary army as a lieutenant-colonel under the Earl of Stamford.[6] He first came to Gloucester as deputy governor in December 1642 and was made governor in the following year.

He was clearly a superb tactician – possibly best seen in his harrying after the siege – and could be very wily. After he captured Monmouth in September 1644 he sent the Welsh prisoners home 'everyone with a little note directed to his master, or to the parish where he lived, to signify to them "That the intention of the Parliament, and of Massey in coming thither, was not to destroy or enslave their persons, or take away their goods or livelihoods; but to preserve their lives and fortunes, to open the cause of justice, and free them of their heavy burdens under the forces of Rupert, a German". By which artifice, and free discharge of the prisoners, the Welsh people began to entertain better thoughts of the Parliament's party than formerly.'[7]

The contemporary parliamentary press quickly awarded him hero status. *Mercurius Civicus* described him in August 1644 as 'that ever renouned and valiant Commander Col. Massey whose valorous achievements were wont formerly to be the subject of almost every pen, and to fill the whole city and kingdom with pleasing discourse'.[8]

Before the start of the siege, Corbet gives him the main credit for maintaining morale. 'Chiefly the hearts of the people were to be held up, wherefore the governor appeared in publicke, rode from place to place with a cheerful aspect, and bearing before him no change in the sudden alteration of fortune.'[9] Essex praised his military abilities in misleading the enemy over his poor strength: 'he managed his business with so much judgement and courage, that the enemy, not knowing of such want, had but small hopes of attaining their desires'.

The popular adulation masked tensions between himself as a soldier and the local politicians. He was impatient with them and criticized their interference in military matters; he also undoubtedly had a strong ego so that 'he liked no partners in honour'. He became increasingly frustrated after the siege at lack of money and men, and his conflict with the city council. He was probably also irritated that his promised promotion did not materialize. Massey was unhappy with the new committee of 'officers, citizens and country gentlemen' formed to raise taxes for the war.[10] He tried to dissolve it by calling on Parliament to send down a committee 'that might take off the former cares and permit him to look to the well ordering of his forces and the safety of this place.'[11] This Parliament did in September 1643, but under the chairmanship of his rival Thomas Pury. In February 1644 Massey wrote to Col. Harley 'Sir, I have understood that there is mischiefe hatching against me and the same promoting here also'.[12] Massey really wanted a clear statement of his overall authority. In October 1644 he wrote 'There is a manifest inconsistency between the settlement of the militia and the disposal of money being in two men's power. The militia cannot stir but when the Committee pleases and approves the design'.[13] He wanted his authority as governor (originally granted as a commission from the Earl of Essex rather than from Parliament) confirmed 'so that my authority may no longer be in question or dispute'.

Massey even tried to take the matter personally to Parliament which won him few friends there. His surprise visit was followed by an order of October 1644 from Parliament 'that no governor of any garrison in the kingdom, or officer in any garrison do presume to come up to the parliament without leave of this house'. Later, in February 1645, he was still making the same complaints, writing to Parliament after Col. Stephens had got himself besieged at Rourdon House, 'I hope the commands may be settled, for independent officers, as I may call them, promise not advantage, but destruction'.[14] By return, Pury tried to remove Massey's staff officers as 'supernumaries'.[15] In March 1645 he wrote to Col. Harley over the influence of Pury on Parliament and their 'hocus pocus juggling'.[16] But such complaints seem to have been borne out of personal antagonisms rather than out of any party differences.

He eventually left Gloucester in June 1645 to become commander of the Western Association, with mixed reaction from the city and county committees. His fate took a critical turn in July 1646 when he became an MP (for Wooton Bassett). Thereafter, like many others, he was caught up in the politics between Parliament and the commanders of the New Model Army – religiously divided between Presbyterians and Independents. His brigade was disbanded in October 1646 and he was removed from army command (along with, among others, his friend Sir William Waller) under the *Self Denying Ordinance*. The often fragile unity of the parliamentary forces was breaking up and the former hero was described by his opponents in the Independent Party as 'a profane man, and unfit for command'.[17] Parliament tried to reappoint him along with other former officers of the Earl of Essex to raise an army as part of the 'Committee of Safety' to defend London against the threat of the New Model Army, but the attempt failed and in June 1647 he was impeached along with other Presbyterian officers.

He managed to flee to Holland but returned again in September 1648 when he voted with the peace party. He was excluded from Parliament in December under 'Pride's Purge' and was then imprisoned. However, he escaped to the continent in January 1649 and then, finally disillusioned with the parliamentary cause and what he saw as his personal betrayal, he offered his services to Prince Charles.

His previous role in helping to defeat Prince Charles's father was politely overlooked. In January 1649 he was in Scotland with Charles II at his coronation at Scone and was placed as second in command of a cavalry regiment with the rank of lieutenant-general. He fought Cromwell in the Scottish campaigns of that year, including the battle of Inverkeithing in July, but was back on the continent by September. Back in Breda, he and other Presbyterian officers dined with the Royalist Richard Watson. Watson's letter gives an indication of the uneasy alliance between the newcomer Presbyterian 'rogues' and those who had remained loyal to the Royalist cause throughout the war. 'They all pretended their good meaning to the murdered king. I asked them why they did not shew it, when it was in their power? . . . The Presbyterians have cozened the kingdom, the Independents the Presbyterians, and the Cavalier must have his turn to cozen one or both; or else there never can be peace.'[18] Massey's part in the further events of the Third Civil War was a succession of secret missions, captures and quite remarkable escapes. On the Royalist march down from Scotland in 1651 he was sent a day ahead of the main forces in order to rally support for Charles II. He was then badly wounded at Upton on Severn before the battle of Worcester when 'at least forty carbines were shot at him within half pistol shot'. These resulted in 'a very dangerous wound that tore his arm and hand in such a manner that he was in great torment, and could not stir out of his bed, in a time when his activity and industry was most useful'.[19] His survival seems to reflect either the poor aim of his adversaries or the effectiveness of his body armour. Eventually he was forced to surrender himself to the wife of his former patron, the Earl of Stamford. Despite promises of good behaviour he escaped but was recaptured and was sent to the Tower of London. However, he escaped once again and went to France.

In 1654 he was back in England as an agent for Charles II. Gloucester was still seen as his potential power base in the event of any rising and he narrowly escaped capture after being recognized by one of his former soldiers who was now an innkeeper at Henton. But the situation seemed hopeless for the Royalists at that time and in 1655 he was driven to seek for work abroad as a mercenary again, travelling to Denmark but with no result. In the autumn of 1656 he was once again plotting in England.

The situation in England now began to change rapidly, and in a supreme irony it was suggested to Charles II in 1659 (after the death of Oliver Cromwell and the succession of his son, Richard as Lord Protector) that, Massey might now be able to capture Gloucester for the Royalists. Its strategic importance was as great then as it had been in 1643 and there were now psychological aspects to consider. Clarendon wrote on 9 May 1659 that few things would be more auspicious for the Royalist cause

> than to hear that Gloucester is defended for the king by Massey; which would look like one of those revolutions which providence brings about, when it will wonderfully restore a prince and people to happiness.[20]

He therefore returned to the city where Royalist accounts suggest that the then mayor, Toby Jordan (one of those who had delivered the city's reply to the surrender demand of 1643), was implicated. Jordan survived the purge of the council in 1662 and was rewarded with the post of coroner. Massey tried to raise the support of gentry in the Forest of Dean, hoping to raise 3,000 men, but his plans were betrayed by Sir Richard Willis and he was captured at Symonds Hall. Although bound on a horse behind a trooper he escaped after the horse stumbled going down Nympsfield Hill!

Finally, Massey did at last return to Gloucester in April 1660 when, despite the opposition of some of the local garrison, he was elected as a city MP. The day before the election he had been invited to dine with the mayor and had attended a church service in St Nicholas's church, but afterwards he was attacked by 'severall of the inferiour Officers (one a Captain) crying out, Fall on, kill the Rogues'. Massey was rescued by the mayor and Corporation. He was thus able to take his seat in the Parliament that restored Charles II. Massey was knighted for his efforts and appointed Governor of Jamaica. He died in 1673 or 1674.

Expenditure on the Defences

Charges Generall for the Fortifications

AN EXTRACT FROM THE CITY CHAMBERLAIN'S ACCOUNTS [1]

Imprimis Payd Jn DOWNE carpenter & TROW for 2 dayes worked att the Westgate	0 – 2 – 8.
Item payd for Two dayes worke att the Blyndgate	0 – 2 – 8.
Item payd xxv labourers for the rate of them a day at the Beareland ditch	1 – 1 – 0.
Item payd Richard HAYNE for a peece of Timber att the Blyndgate	0 – 2 – 8.
Item payd xij workmen att the Beareland ditch for rate of them a daye	0 – 10 – 0.
Item payd xiiij workmen att the Beareland ditch for each of them a daye	0 – 11 – 8.
Item payd xij workmen att the Bareland ditch rate of them a day	0 – 10 – 0.
Item payd BARNELIND for 5 powthen hornis for the ordinance	0 – 4 – 6.
Item payd WILSTEED for 216 pike for the turnepike	1 – 8 – 6.
Item payd John & Richard STEEPHINS for theyr worke & given Timber for the Turne Pyke	1 – 4 – 6.
Item payd John WILSTEED iiij pickeaxes	0 – 6 – 0.
Item payd Two workemen for making an end of the ditch att the Beareland rate of them a day	0 – 1 – 8.
Item payd for CHARTEABRE for mending & putting in the Staples att the Northgate	0 – 0 – 8.
Item payd for mending Two shoville vd & for naylis iiijd	0 – 0 – 9.

Item payd Thomas WATTERSON for paving at the Three Cocks porcullis & Archdeacons Lane	0 – 1 – 0.
Item payd for xxij Clubbs iijs viijd & for 2 spitting shovells ijs iiijd for helvyng Two pickaxes & mending 2 shovells viijd	0 – 6 – 8.
Item payd John DOWNE carpenter for 6 dayes worke att the severall gates & Turnepike	0 – 8 – 0.
Item payd HAYNE & his man for sawynge	0 – 5 – 10.
Item payd HAYNE for 2 tonn & halfe & 9 foote of Timber	3 – 6 – 0.
Item payd him for a planke	0 – 2 – 8.
Item payd CHURCHE ye carpenter and his man for vj dayes a peece xiiijs payd him for 2 peyces of Timber xxs	1 – 14 – 0.
Item payd for hawlinge of Tymber to the Westgate	0 – 0 – 8.
Item payd LOGGYINS the mason for halfe a dayes worke att the Northgate	0 – 0 – 8.
Item payd for a pole vjd & for helving 2 pyckaxes viiijd	0 – 0 – 10.
Item payd Rodger ESTOPP for helping about the Ordinance	0 – 2 – 6.
Item payd for Two dossen of Clubbes	0 – 4 – 0.
Item payd for Naylis used at Alvyngate	0 – 0 – 6.
Item payd Mr ELLIS for his expence in bringing the Ordinance as appeares by his note & order	5 – 13 – 7.
Item payd for Naylis used att the Posternegate iiijd payd for xx foote of Elme boords used there xxd	0 – 2 – 0.
Item payd WALTERE for cleansing the brooke att Alvyngate	0 – 2 – 0.
Item payd Peter CHEWETT for iiij dayes iiijs viijd And WmTURNER for vj dayes viijs pd for helpe to hang Alvingate	0 – 13 – 0.
Item payd Wm TROW for five dayes vjs viijd & Thomas MORGAN for iiij dayes iiijs & iijd for nayles used at Alvingate	0 – 11 – 7.
Item payd Edward DOWNE for severall journeys & horse hyor as appeares by note & order	1 – 16 – 0.
Item payd for hawling of Timber to the severall gates	0 – 2 – 4.
Item payd Nicholas WILLIAMS for making cariedges for the Ordinances	0 – 3 – 4.

178

Item payd 13 laburers att Dockam	0 – 10 – 0.
Item payd iiij labourers at Dockam	0 – 4 – 0.
Item payd sixteene labourers att Dockam at 10d a day	0 – 13 – 4.
Item payd for Shydes (planks) used there xijd for naylis 1d	0 – 1 – 1.
Item payd Jn WELSTEED for xij pickaxes & 57 at 3d ob	0 – 16 – 8.
Item payd George MALLETTS for Wyar used about the Ordinance	0 – 0 – 4.
Item paydd for six lynestocke & a forme to COSBY	0 – 2 – 0.
Item payd PAYNE for xij foote of boord used at the Northgate and for 2 plankes used at Dockam ijs & for hawling timber there	0 – 3 – 0.
Item pd Richard BEALEN for 31 lb Lead to make aprones for the Ordinance	0 – 3 – 10.
Item payd PEGLER for Two payre of wheeles for the Ordinance	2 – 2 – 0.
Item payd Thomas ALDREDGE for plankes for the postern & the Northgate as appeares by Note	0 – 17 – 4.
Item payd the hawlyer for hawling the Ordinances and for labourers to helpe about them	0 – 3 – 0.
Item payd Thomas WATTERSON and his sonn for pavynge about the Postes att the severall gates	0 – 2 – 2.
Item payd Mr FOWLER that hee layed out for fower Clubbs	0 – 0 – 8.
Item payd Mr Henry ELLICE for viij dosen of Clubbs which hee laid out	0 – 16 – 8.
Item payd him more for Two skynes for sponges for the Ordinance	0 – 2 – 6.
Item payd for hawling upp of Matche to the Tolsey ijd and for – [RA . . .] ijd	0 – 0 – 4.
Item payd Thomas WATTERSON & his sonne for a dayes worke for pavyng about the Southgate postes & att other gates	0 – 2 – 2.
Item payd Walter NICHOLLS for three dayes worke for his man for putting in Crampes for the chaynes at the gates	0 – 4 – 0.
Item payd for hawling of Timber from Alvyngate	0 – 0 – 4.
Item payd Moses BEATON for halfe cwt 15lb of lead	0 – 8 – 10.

Item payd for nayles used att the South East & Northgates	$0 - 5 - 7^{1}/_{2}$.
Item payd Jn WELSTEED for a chayne for Alvyngate cont. 60 [?] at $3^{1}/_{2}$	$0 - 17 - 6$.
Item payd him for a chayne for the Northgatee at 94 (?) at $3^{1}/_{2}$	$1 - 7 - 5$.
Item payd Wm WOODWARD for putting fferrells & pykes in the Lynestock	$0 - 9 - 3$.
Item payd Wm SHIPTON for Strakes for a payre of wheeles $100^{1}/_{2}$ & 18 lbs at 3d a lb	$2 - 6 - 6$.
Item payd for putting them on	$0 - 1 - 0$.
Item payd Anthony MOTLEY for a lanthorne for the watch att Alvyngate	$0 - 2 - 0$.
Item payd Jn MELL for $100^{1}/_{2}$ of large doore nayles used att the posternegate	$0 - 5 - 0$.
Item payd Peter RICKE for putting upp the Chaynes at Alvyngate	$0 - 0 - 3$.
Item payd the Widow WOODLEY for 5 faggotts	$0 - 0 - 4$.
Item payd for hawlinge halfe a thousand of bricks & a barrell of lyme of Master OSBOURNE's gate	$0 - 1 - 8$.
Item payd Edward WOOD for halfe a thousand of bricks used there	$0 - 3 - 8$.
Item payd Jn KIRKUM and Thomas WOODWARD for worke done by them att the gates & for a chayne as by their note appears	$6 - 7 - 3$.
Item payd Walter NICHOLLS for a day & halfe for putting in the staples att the Northgate	$0 - 2 - 0$.
Item payd for fowre Kinderkynns to put the cartridges in	$0 - 6 - 0$.
Item payd Robert CINGLEY for hawling the Ordinance out of St Michaelles church	$0 - 0 - 8$.
Item payd for xiij Ells & $^{3}/_{4}$ of canvas to make cartridges	$0 - 16 - 0$.
Item payd for three Quyre of white paper for cartridges	$0 - 1 - 9$.
Item payd for Starch Needles packthreed & browne threed used about the cartridges xiiijd & pd for a pownde & $^{1}/_{2}$ sope used about the wheeles	$0 - 1 - 7$.
Item payd for xiiij powndes of hurdes [?] iiijs And iij lbs $^{1}/_{4}$ of rapworth yearne xvjd And payd Jn EVANS for a double belth rope ijs for arming of the shotts	$0 - 7 - 4$.
Item payd HATTON att severall tymes helping	

about the Ordinance before hee entered into

ther paye .... 0 – 5 – 7.

Item payd for 2 baggs of charcoalis for putting in
the draines att the Westgate viijd Pd Walter
NICHOLLS for his man for putting in the
Crampes one day & ¹/₂ there ijs .... 0 – 2 – 8.

Item payd Jn TOMPKINS for worke done att
severall places and att the gates. And also a
large chayne for the Eastgate .... 6 – 15 – 8.

Item payd WOODLEY for hawling upp the
Ammunition to Mr HATHERWAYES .... 0 – 0 – 4.

Item payd Edward STURNUYE for covering iiij
kinderkinns with leather for the cartridges .... 0 – 8 – 0.

Item payd Mr Lawrence SINGLETON for halfe
a hundred boards to make wheelbarrows .... 0 – 3 – 0.

Item payd for the hawling of two poasts from
the windlise 4d And for hawling the Ordinance
from the Wheatmarket to the Barleymarkett iiijs ... 0 – 4 – 4.

Item payd Wm WOODWARD for worke done att
the severall gates and for the Turnepykes & for
chaynes & shott & other things as by his note
appears .... 14- 12 – 0.

Item payd Mr Steward GREENE for what hee
disburst in his & Edward WHEELERS foundry.

Item payd to Mr Steward FfOWLER and for his
horse hyor when hee went to the Lord SAYE ...... 1 – 0 – 8.

Item payd him more that hee payd him for locks
to Mr HATHERWAY & other things as by his note
appears .... 1 – 13 – 8.

Item payd him more that hee payd out for me
and for his horse to Mr Ald. PURYE .... 0 – 2 – 10.

Item payd Mr Ald PURYE & Mr Ald
SINGLETON for their expence in theyr journey to Worcester ... 1 – 6 – 0.

Item payd Walter PINKE for soe much layed out
by him and for mending the locke att Alvingate ... 0 – 1 – 0.

Item payd Mr Ald SINGLETON for Iron
delivered unto certain Smiths for the cittyes use ... 10 – 0 – 0.

Item payd CRUMPE for his journey when hee
went upp to London to the Parliament
concerning the Earle of Worcester his horses
which were stayed here .... 1 – 10 – 0.

Item payd for the hyor of a horse the note
Mr WOOD has two journeys about Musketts neare Cheapstow ... 0 – 6 – 0.

Item payd Thomas ELDREDGE for iij pullyes
Two double ones & one single one .... 0 – 4 – 6.

Item payd him for 42 cartridges ijd $^1/_2$ a peece	0 – 8 – 9.
Item payd for two turned peeces for springs	0 – 0 – 4.
Item payd him for Two Rommes	0 – 0 – 4.
Item payd him for one staffe ix foote longe	0 – 1 – 6.
Item payd him for helving vj great Mattocks	0 – 1 – 6.
Item payd him for helvinge xiij lesser mattocks	0 – 2 – 2.
Item payd Robert LONGDEN for two spitting shovells	0 – 2 – 4.
Item payd Augustyne GREENE for halfe a hundred of boards less three foote used at the Southgate	0 – 4 – 3.
Item payd for ELLIS 3 quart of canvas to make cartridges	0 – 4 – 10.
Item payd for taking down a scaffold & placing the boards by Mr Ald. SINGLETON's order.	0 – 2 – 6.

One of the most interesting of the city accounts lists a number of items of expenditure on the defences during 1642–3, totalling £93 0s 11$^1/_2$d in all, of which the above is an extract.

Civilian skills were being put to good use as the medieval gates were being repaired by masons and carpenters. As well as the timber and nails, bricks were also used in large quantities to make good the old stonework. The Alvin Gate itself was re-hung and chains installed across others.

Labourers at work in the ditch at Bareland (Bearland) were also cleaning out the brook at the Alvin Gate, reinforcing the suggestion that the natural stream courses were used in the defences on the east side of the town. A large number of men were also engaged at Dockam. Although there is no proof, it is possible that they were preparing wooden sluices ready to flood the meadows on the north and north-west side of the town.

Everyday tools were bought for the job – pickaxes, spitting shovels (clay spades), mallets for wire 'used about the ordinance'. The work took its toll and some shovels needed mending. A new fleet of wheelbarrows was made to carry the soil out of the ditches to be piled up as ramparts or to line the back of the medieval wall.

The list also includes items of more obvious military connection. Over 200 pikes were bought to build turnpikes across the approach roads. These were intended to hinder cavalry charges. Artillery was to be of key importance during the siege. Though other accounts tell of the purchase of guns it is clear that the citizens themselves had to make up some of the necessary equipment, sometimes collecting scrap iron for the purpose. They had to make gun carriages and find lead to make protective aprons beside the cannon. The artillery positions were not static and wheels had to be made for the gun carriages and soap provided to oil them. Payments were made for moving the artillery around as from Wheat Market to Barley Market and out of St Michael's church. There are also references to the ancillary equipment needed to fire the cannon. The accounts include powder horns to load the priming powder into the touch hole, linstocks which were long poles with metal pike-like head clamp and ferrule used to carry the slow-burning match which was used to ignite the powder in the touch-hole to fire the cannon, skins for sponges to clean the barrels out after firing. The powder for the main charge of the cannons appears to have been prepared in advance within paper and canvas cartridges sewn up with thread. These were kept in the 18 gallon barrels (Kinderkynns), some covered with leather to help keep them waterproof. Payments to foundries may include the manufacture of shot. The references to ropes in connection with the ordinance may be to provide the ropes used to hold the carriages steady but the 'double belt rope' may have been to arm the 'great crossbow' that the city obtained.

There was also a citizen army to equip. Mr Wood was sent out to find muskets around Chepstow. The most common type used during the Civil War was the matchlock, with the charge set of using a slow-burning fuse or match. But flintlocks (firelocks) were also used, initially provided for guards of magazines or artillery where the continuously lighted match would have posed a great fire risk. They were particularly useful to siege garrisons as matchlocks could use up enormous amounts of the match referred to in the above accounts. One thousand five hundred men might use 5 cwt of match a day. Thus the 'locks' bought by Mr Hatherway may refer to flintlocks. If the flintlock was the height of seventeenth-century military invention then at the other end of the technical scale were the simple wooden clubs bought at 2d each.

The names referred to in the accounts feature several well-known citizens. Most notable was the interest payment for a horse to Thomas Pury. The 'rogue' cannoneer Hatton, who later deserted, is also mentioned – here being paid 5s 7d for helping 'about the ordinance' before he joined the army.

Notes

LIST OF ABBREVIATIONS

Clarendon   Edward Earl of Clarendon, *The History of the Rebellion and Civil Wars in England* (ed. W. Dunn Macray, 1888)

Corbet   J. Corbet, *The Historical Relation of the Military Government of Gloucester* (1645). Glos. Colln 9125. Reprinted in Washbourn, pp. 1–152

CSPD   *Calendar of State Papers (Domestic)*

Dorney   (1643) J. Dorney, *A Brief and Exact Relation of the most mate riall and remarkable passages that hapned in the late well-formed (and as valiently defended) seige laid before Gloucester* (1643). Glos. Colln 2.5. Republished in Washbourn, pp.207–32

Dorney (1653)   J. Dorney, *Certain Speeches made upon the day of the yearly election* (1653). Glos. Colln 6059

Dorney   Fosbrooke T.D. Fosbrooke, *An Original History of the City of Gloucester* (Gloucester, 1819). Reprint, Alan Sutton 1976

Foster   H. Foster, *A True and Exact Relation of the marchings of the two regiments of the trained bands of the City of London . . . who marched forth for the reliefe of the city of Gloucester* (1643). Republished in Washbourn, 253–71

GBR   Gloucester Borough Records in GRO

Glos. Colln   The Gloucestershire Collection of printed works and manuscripts in Gloucester Divisional Library

GNQ   *Gloucestershire Notes and Queries*

GRO   Gloucestershire Records Office

HMC   Historical Manuscripts Commission *12th Report, Appendix IX* (1891)

Journal   'A Journal of the Siege of Gloucester', *GNQ* 3 (1887), pp. 437–9

PRO   Public Record Office
TBGAS   *Trans. Bristol and Glos. Archaeol. Soc.*
Washbourn   J. Washbourn, *Bibliotheca Gloucestrensis* (Gloucester, 1825)
VCH   *Victoria County History of the County of Gloucester. Vol.IV The
           City of Gloucester*, ed. N.M. Herbert (Oxford, 1988)

INTRODUCTION

1. *Lady Fanshawe's Memoirs,* quoted in M.B. Osborne, *Cromwellian Fortifications in Cambridgeshire,* 1990, p.1.
2. Glos. Colln 8326 (25); republished in Washbourn, pp.253–71.
3. Journal, pp.437–9.
4. PRO SP28 129/5.
5. S. Lysons, *The Romans in Gloucestershire* (Gloucester, 1860), p.50 and map.
6. First discussed in detail in M. Atkin, 'The Civil War Defences of Gloucester', *Fortress*, 10 (1991), pp.32–8.

CHAPTER 1. BACKGROUND TO WAR

1. T. Rudge, *History and Antiquities of Gloucester from the Earliest Period to the Present Time* (Gloucester, 1811), pp.151–2.
2. GBR 1406/1521, f.195.
3. J. Langton, 'Late Medieval Gloucester: some data from a rental of 1455', *Trans. Inst. Brit. Geogr.* 2 (1977), fn.13.
4. M. Richards, 'Massey's house', MS in GRO.
5. Surveyed by F.W. Charles in 1976. Notes, drawings and photographs in Gloucester Building Record (copy at Gloucester Folk Museum).
6. P. Ripley, 'Poverty in Gloucester and its Alleviation', *TBGAS* 103 (1985), p.186.
7. Thanks to Nigel Spry (who excavated this site on behalf of the Gloucester and District Archaeological Research Group) for this information in advance of publication.
8. W.H. Stephenson (ed.), *Calendar of the Records of the Corporation of Gloucester* (Gloucester, 1893), p.15.
9. GBR B3/2, ff.340–1.
10. As listed in the trades referred to under the Muster of 1608: J. Smith

Men and Armour (1902; 2nd edn, Alan Sutton, 1980), pp.2–10.
11. A.G. Vince, 'Post-medieval pottery' in C.M. Heighway, *The East and North Gates of Gloucester* (Western Archaeological Trust, 1983), pp.138–40.
12. HMC pp.476–7; GBR H 2/2, pp.67, 131.
13. J.K.G. Taylor, 'The Civil Government of Gloucester, 1640–6', *TBGAS* 67 (1946), Appendix 1.

CHAPTER 2. GLOUCESTER TAKES SIDES

1. Corbet, p.41.
2. Draft orders for the reduction of the city of Gloucester. From the papers of Sir Edward Walker, Secretary of State for War: Glos. Colln JF 2.1.
3. Clarendon III, pp.516–17.
4. M. Ashley, *The English Civil War* (revised edn Gloucester, 1990), p.2.
5. Corbet, p.139.
6. Letter of 22 March 1645 to Sir Samuel Luke published in J. and T.W. Webb (eds), 'A military memoir of Colonel John Birch', *Camden Society* 7 (1873), pp.216–17.
7. Glos. Colln 3166 (9); A. Fletcher, *The Outbreak of the English Civil War* (London, 1981), pp.387–8.
8. Corbet, pp.9–10, 16–17.
9. Draft orders issued by Charles I for military operations in Gloucestershire. From the papers of Sir Edward Walker, Secretary of State for War: Glos. Colln JF 2.1.
10. Washbourn, Appendix IV.
11. Corbet, p.68.
12. Corbet, p.16.
13. Corbet, p.10.
14. Corbet, p.8.
15. Corbet, p.17.
16. *CSPD* 1650, 27 June 1650, p.218.
17. B. Manning, *The English People and the English Revolution* (London, 1991), p.333.
18. C.E. Hart, *Royal Forest* (Oxford, 1966), pp.125–30.
19. Corbet, p.39.
20. J. Roland Phillips, *Civil War in Wales and the Marches* (London, 1874), p.139.

21. Washbourn, note 220, clxxvii.
22. Richard Baxter, a friend of Corbet and Dorney, quoted in Washbourn, xxii.
23. GBR B 3/2, f.172.
24. Glos. Colln JF4.13; *VCH*, p.92.
25. HMC 14th Report, Duke of Portland MSS vol.III, Appendix II (HMSO, 1894), pp.125–6.
26. Quoted in G.M. Trevelyan, *England under the Stuarts* (London, 1904), p.192.
27. *Certain Special Passages* 15–23 August 1642, quoted in Fosbrooke, p.27.
28. Dorney (1643), p.210.

CHAPTER 3. THE OUTBREAK OF WAR

1. *Perfect Diurnal*, 29 August to 5 September 1642, quoted in Fosbrooke, p.27.
2. Corbet, p.11.
3. J.K.G. Taylor, 'The Civil Government of Gloucester, 1640–6', *TBGAS* 67 (1946), pp.67 and 76. The Committee for Defence was established 5 August 1642 but may have been dissolved in July 1643 and replaced by later 'Committees to survey the works'.
4. Corbet, p.22.
5. Ibid.
6. Corbet, pp.23–4.
7. *Strange Discoveries, or Continuation of certain special and remarkable passeages* No.36, quoted in Fosbrooke, p.30.
8. *CSPD* 1641–3, 6 February 1643, p.442, No.22.
9. *Perfect Diurnal*, 20–27 February 1643, quoted in Fosbrooke, pp.28–9.
10. *A famous victory obtained by . . . Sir William Waller . . . at Padsworth Printed Feb 25 1643*. Glos. Colln 10952 (3).
11. *Perfect Diurnal*, 6–13 March 1643, quoted in Fosbrooke, pp.29–30.
12. GBR B3/2, f.245 for 6 March 1643.
13. *Mercurius Aulicus*, 12 February 1643, quoted in Fosbrooke, p.29.
14. Corbet, p.27. The Town regiment was not formed until April and Dennis Wise was not listed among its officers by Dorney.
15. Roland Phillips 1874 (chap.2, note 20), p.66.
16. Excavations by Richard Bryant in 1978. Information on the clay pipes

from Allan Peacey, with thanks.

17. Furney MS in Bodleian Library published in Washbourn, Appendix II, p.372.
18. GBR B3/2, f.271.
19. Corbet, pp.40–1.
20. GBR H2/3, f.27.
21. Washbourn, cxxxix (note 23).
22. Corbet, p.11.
23. GBR B3/2, f.205.
24. GBR B3/2, f.221 for 5 August 1642.
25. Taylor 1946 (note 3), Appendix 1.
26. Lords Journals 14 January 1643; Washbourn, cxxxix.
27. GBR B3/2, f.245.
28. Corbet, pp.25–6.
29. GBR B3/2, ff. 235, 236 for 19 November 1642; Draft Minute Book f.194, GBR B3/2, f.317 for 6 October 1644.
30. GBR B3/2, f.253.
31. GBR B3/2, f.240.
32. Ibid.
33. GBR B3/2, ff.248 and 250 for 7 and 21 March 1643.
34. GBR B3/2, f.249 for 11 March 1643.
35. Taylor 1946 (note 3), p.86.
36. GBR B3/2, ff.247–8.
37. GBR B3/2, f.237.
38. Corbet, p.37.
39. Corbet, p.22.
40. GBR B3/2, f.254 for 15 April 1643.
41. Corbet, p.21.
42. Clarendon, p.79.
43. Bodleian Library, Wood Pamphlets 376.35.
44. Clarendon II, p. 979.
45. British Library Harley MSS 1608, f.114.
46. GBR B3/2, f.251.
47. GBR B3/2, f.245 for 1 March 1643.
48. British Library Harley MSS 6804, f.118.
49. Bodleian Library Tanner MSS 62, ff.199–200.
50. Bodleian Library Tanner MSS 62, f.197; but cf. Corbet in Washbourn, p.40.

51. Corbet, p.40.
52. Corbet, p.41.
53. PRO SP28 129/5 C11. Money paid on 7–10 August to Captains Nelme, Evans, Pury, Nurse and Singleton of the Town regiment, and Colonel Forbes and Massey. I am grateful to Russell Howes for bringing these accounts to my attention and for giving access to his notes.
54. Journal, p.438.
55. *Mercurius Aulicus* No.34 quoted in Fosbrooke, 46.
56. Clarendon II, p. 471.
57. Dorney (1643), p.218.
58. Clarendon III, p.512.
59. *Perfect Diurnal*, 28 August to 4 September 1643, quoted in Fosbrooke, pp.42–3.
60. Corbet, p.50.
61. *Certain Informations from severall parts of the Kingdom* No.36, 18–25 September: British Library Thomason Tracts.
62. PRO SP28 228 Commonwealth Exchequer Rolls.
63. *A True Relation of the severall passages which have happened to our army since it advanced towards Gloucester* (14 September 1643) in Washbourn, p.280.

CHAPTER 4. THE SIEGE OF 1643: DEFENCES

1. F.A. Hyett, *Gloucester in National History* (Gloucester, 1906), p.103.
2. Letter of Lord Herbert, Marquis of Worcester, to Charles II,1666–7, HMC, 60.
3. GRO Hyett Colln 667.16(2).
4. Clarendon II, p.475.
5. *CSPD* 1641–3, 25 August 1643, p.479, No.151.
6. GBR B3/2, ff.244 and 250. Nicholas Devereux was a cousin of the Earl of Essex. He was only a captain during the period of the siege but received his colonel's commission on 12 September.
7. Fosbrooke, p.69.
8. Journal, pp.437–9.
9. *A Continuation of Certain Speciall and Remarkable Passages informed to Parliament* 20–27 July 1643: British Library Thomason Tracts.
10. Bodleian Library Tanner MSS 62, ff.199–200.
11. Corbet, pp.42–3.

12. Clarendon II, p.475.

13. Site 3/84: A.P. Garrod, 'Site Reports', *Glevensis* 19 (1985), p.47.

14. H. O'Neil, 'Friars Orchard, Technical College, Gloucester, 1961', *TBGAS* 81 (1962), p.13.

15. Site 46/74: C.M. Heighway, *The East and North Gates of Gloucester* (Western Archaeological Trust, 1983), p.60.

16. H. O'Neil, 'Gloucester Roman Research Committee Report 1931–2', *TBGAS* 53 (1931), p.28 and fig.6, pp.68–9.

17. Corbet, p.51.

18. A. Saunders, *Fortress Britain* (Liphook, 1989), p.72.

19. Site 3/83: A.P. Garrod, 'Site Reports', *Glevensis* 18 (1984), p.48.

20. Dorney (1643), p.211.

21. Washbourn, op. cit. in note 2, p.216: present author's italics.

22. Corbet, p.52.

23. Ibid., pp.47, 51.

24. Site 23/82: information pers. comm. A.P. Garrod, with thanks.

25. A.P. Garrod, 'Site Notes', *Glevensis* 17 (1983), p.31.

26. Excavations on site 13/83 (Southgate Gallery) in 1983 by C. Guy and on sites 36/88 (Bank of England) and 3/89 (Southgate Gallery) in 1988 and 1989 by M. Atkin.

27. Dorney (1643), p.214.

28. Ibid., pp.215–17.

29. Ibid., p.217.

30. Dorney (1887), pp.464–6.

31. Dorney (1643), p.224.

32. Site 2/90: P. Greatorex, 'Archaeological observations on the Eastgate Street sewer renewal 1990', in M. Atkin *et al.*, 'Archaeological field-work in Gloucester 1990', *Glevensis* 25 (1991), pp. 28–9.

33. HMC, p.507.

34. Dorney (1643), p.211.

35. Ibid., p.224.

36. Royal Commission on Historic Monuments 1964. Newark-on-Trent: *The Civil War Siegeworks* (HMSO, London, 1964), p.32.

37. Dorney (1643), p.212.

38. Quoted in P. Gaunt, *A Nation Under Siege* (HMSO, 1991), p.34.

39. Site 36/88: M. Atkin, 'Excavations in Gloucester 1988: an interim report', *Glevensis* 23 (1989), pp.7–11; 'Excavations in Gloucester 1989: an interim report', *Glevensis* 24 (1990), p.3.

40. Site 3/89: M. Atkin, 'Excavations in Gloucester 1989: an interim report', *Glevensis* 24 (1990), pp.3–7.
41. Furney MS quoted in Fosbrooke, p.139.
42. GBR F4/5, ff.326–7, f.226, f.254.
43. PRO SP28 129/5 C11.
44. Letter of 4 June 1643 from General Waller to Lady Scudamore, published in T.W. Webb (ed.), 'A Military Memoir of Colonel John Birch', *Camden Society* 7 (1873), pp.204–5.
45. GBR B3/2, f.266 for 20 June 1643.
46. Dorney (1643), p.211.
47. Grand Inquest of 1646 quoted in Fosbrooke, pp.70–1.
48. GBR F4/5, f.326.
49. GBR F4/4, f.252.
50. Corbet, p.45.
51. Ordinance of 1648 quoted in Washbourn, p.360; GBR G3/502 for January 1645.
52. GBR F4/5, f.242.
53. GBR F4/5, f.366.
54. S. Rudder, *New History of Gloucestershire* (Gloucester, 1779), p.172.
55. British Library Burney Colln, *Mercurius Britanicus* 3rd to 10th November 1645, quoted in Stoyle *The Civil War defences of Exeter and the great parliamentary siege of 1645–46* (Exeter Museums Archaeological Field Unit, 1990), p.16.
56. GBR H2/3, ff.136–7 for 27 November 1651.
57. See Appendix 2; GBR F 4/5, ff.179–94.
58. Washbourn, pp.11, 48.
59. I am grateful to A.P. Garrod for much discussion on the evidence of Civil War activity in Kingsholm, based on the results of his various watching briefs.
60. Site 10/89: by A.P. Garrod. See M. Atkin and A.P Garrod, 'Archaeology in Gloucester 1989: a review', *TBGAS* 108 (1990), p.189.
61. Site 19/91: by M. Atkin.
62. Dorney (1643), p.227.
63. Fosbrooke, p.71.
64. Ordinance of 1644.
65. GBR B3/2, f.273 for 29 August 1643.
66. GBR B3/2, f.226.

67. GBR G3/SR, 1445/1567.

68. HMC, p.503.

69. In November 1644 the Justices had to issue an order to try to prevent soldiers from 'tippling' when they should have been on duty: Draft Minute Book, f.34b.

70. GBR F4/5, f.192.

71. GBR F4/5, f.189.

72. PRO SP 28 129/5.

CHAPTER 5. THE SIEGE OF 1643: TACTICS

1. *Perfect Diurnal*, 28 August to 4 September 1643, quoted in Fosbrooke, p. 43.

2. *Mercurius Britanicus* 2, 29 August–5 September. Glos. Colln 7888.9.

3. Clarendon II, p.511.

4. *Eikon Basilike* (ed. P.A. Knachel, 1966), pp.38–9.

5. Trial of Nathaniel Fiennes quoted in Washbourn, xlviii.

6. Bodleian Library Tanner MSS 62, f.197.

7. Clarendon II, p.474.

8. Clarendon II, p.475.

9. Dorney (1643), p.222 and p.228.

10. Literally to hammer a spike into the touch hole of a cannon and so making it impossible to fire. Also referred to as 'nailing'.

11. GRO D115, Letter from Charles I, 'Given at our Court at Matson'.

12. Dorney (1887), pp.464–5.

13. Foster, p.261.

14. T. Carlyle, *Letters and Speeches of Oliver Cromwell* (1845), xxxi.

15. S. Bull, *Granadoe!* (Leigh-on-Sea, 1991), p.11.

16. Washbourn, p.261.

17. Dorney (1643), p.216.

18. Dorney (1643), p.214.

19. GBR Stewards Account MS 1642–3.

20. Dorney (1643), p.222.

21. Dorney (1887), pp.464–5.

22. Dorney (1643), p.215.

23. Journal, p.438.

24. Washbourn, clxx.

25. Site 7/76: by A.P. Garrod. See C.M. Heighway, *The East and North*

Gates of Gloucester (Western Archaeological Trust, 1983), pp.39–40.

26. J. Gwynne, *Military Memoirs of the great Civil War* (Cambridge, 1987), p.34.
27. Site 1/91: by M. Walters.
28. Site 36/88: see M. Atkin, 'Excavations in Gloucester 1988: an interim report', *Glevensis* 23 (1989), p.10 and fig.3.
29. Site 21/90: by P. Greatorex.
30. Dorney (1643), p.214.
31. S. Lysons, *The Romans in Gloucestershire* (Gloucester, 1860), p.50.
32. Dorney (1643), p.212.
33. Site 25/89: by A.P. Garrod. I am grateful to A.P. Garrod for this suggestion.
34. Site 11/86: I am grateful to A.P. Garrod for this suggestion. See A.P. Garrod, 'Annual Review of Minor Development Sites In Gloucester', *Glevensis* 21 (1987), p.21.
35. Site 9/83: by A.P. Garrod.
36. Site 3/91: by M. Walters and M. Atkin.
37. I. Philip (ed.), 'Journal of Sir Samuel Luke', *Oxfordshire Record Society* (1950–3), p.138; Corbet, p.54.
38. Dorney (1643), p.225.
39. P. Young and W. Emberton, *Sieges of the Great Civil War 1642–1646* (London, 1978), p.40.
40. Corbet, p.50.
41. Ibid.
42. Corbet, p.53.
43. Corbet, p.45.
44. *Certain Informations from severall parts of the Kingdom* No.34, 4–11 September: British Library Thomason Tracts E67.
45. Clarendon II, p. 512.
46. *Pers. comm.* Charles Garrad, Ontario Archaeology Society, with thanks.
47. Journal, p.438.
48. Dorney (1643), p.222; Journal, p.439.
49. Journal, p.438.
50. Dorney (1643), p.218.
51. Ibid., p.223.
52. Ibid., p.221.
53. Ibid., p.223.
54. Ibid., p.225.

55. *Perfect Diurnal,* 28 August to 4 September 1643, quoted in Fosbrooke, p.43.

56. *Profitable Intelligencer*, 29 June 1644. British Library Thomason Tracts E52.

57. *Perfect Diurnal,* 3 October 1642, quoted in Fosbrooke, p.28.

58. F.A. Hyett, 'A rare Civil War tract', *Archaeol.* J. (1891) xlviii, pp.2–6.

59. *Mercurius Britanicus* 2, 29 August–5 September. British Library Thomason Tracts.

60. Dorney (1887), p.466.

61. Dorney (1643), p.218.

CHAPTER 6. INSIDE THE BESIEGED CITY

1. GBR H2/3, f.133 for 16 December 1651.

2. Dorney (1643), p.217.

3. Dorney (1643), p.215.

4. Corbet, pp.50–1.

5. *A True Relation of the severall passages which have happened to our army since it advanced towards Gloucester with the manner of the relief of the same Sept. 14 1643.* British Library Thomason Tracts E58/23.

6. Corbet, p.48.

7. Corbet, p.48.

8. Dorney (1643), p.221.

9. Furney MS quoted in Washbourn, p.372.

10. HMC, p.507.

11. Dorney (1643), p.220.

12. Ibid., pp.226–8.

13. N. Mayhew and D. Viner, 'A Civil War coin hoard from Weston-sub-Edge, Gloucestershire', *TBGAS* 105 (1987), pp.213–22.

14. Dorney (1643), p.212.

15. Corbet, p.42.

16. Dorney (1643), p.209.

17. *Mercurius Britanicus*, 29 August–5 September: British Library Thomason Tracts.

CHAPTER 7. THE RELIEF OF THE CITY

1. Foster, p.253.

2. Clarendon II, p.514.

3. Letter of 28 August from John Bridges at Warwick Castle to Sir Samuel Luke. Glos. Colln 10952 (22); Calendar of the Committee for the Advance of Money: I am grateful to Russell Howes for this reference.

4. Glos. Colln NF 2.1.

5. Bodleian Library Tanner MSS 62, ff.293–4.

6. Dorney (1643), p.226.

7. *Mercurius Aulicus,* 28 August 1643.

8. Quoted in Roland Phillips 1874 (chap.2, note 20), p.170.

9. Clarendon II, p.542.

10. Clarendon II, p.543.

11. Clarendon II, p.720.

12. *Certain Informations from severall parts of the Kingdom* No.34 4–11 September. British Library Thomason Tracts E67.

13. Dorney (1887), p.466.

14. Clarendon II, p.515.

15. Foster, p.258.

16. Clarendon II, p.542.

17. *A True and Impartial Relation of the Bataille of Newbury*, quoted in Fosbrooke, p.42.

18. Commons Journal 1642–4, 15 September 1643, p.241.

CHAPTER 8. WAR CONTINUES 1644–51

1. *CSPD* 1644–5, 11 November 1644, p.112.

2. *Mercurius Aulicus*, 19 September 1643, quoted in Fosbrooke, p.47.

3. *CSPD* 4 August; 1 and 9 September 1644.

4. *CSPD* 1644–5, 21 January 1645, pp.266–8.

5. *CSPD* 1644–5, 12 February 1645, pp.301–2.

6. *CSPD* 1644–5, 22 January, p.272, No.30.

7. GBR F4/5, f.223 for levelling 'works' outside the walls; GBR B3/2, f.276.

8. GBR F4/5, f.243.

9. GBR F4/5, f.250.

10. GBR B3/2, ff.294, 302.

11. *Perfect Diurnal*, 5 March 1643–4, quoted in Fosbrooke, p.50.

12. *Perfect Occurrences*, 31 May to 7 June 1643–1644, quoted in Fosbrooke, p.51.

13. *Perfect Diurnal,* 29 January to 5 February 1643–1644, quoted in Fosbrooke, p.48.
14. Commons Journal, 12 April 1645.
15. *A True Relation of a wicked plot intended and still on foot against the city of Gloucester 1644*, published in Washbourn, pp.285–324.
16. *CSPD* July 1650, p.248; CSPD 26 October 1650, p.399.
17. Letter of Charles Fleetwood 25 August 1551, published in *Cromwelliana* (1810), p.110.
18. GBR H2/3, f.72.
19. GBR H2/3, f.74.
20. GBR H2/3, f.69 for 20 August 1651.
21. HMC, p.503.
22. GBR H2/3, f.79 for 26 August 1651.
23. GBR H2/3, ff.80–1.
24. HMC, p.504.
25. See Washbourn, Appendix XIA for the raising of additional forces from the town.
26. GBR H2/3, ff.52–5 for 15 April 1651; GBR H2/3, f.60 for May 1651.
27. Site 46/74: by A.P. Garrod.
28. Contra Heighway, *op. cit.*, p.61 and fig.40.
29. Site 14/90: by P. Greatorex.
30. Sites 4/82 and 21/90: by A.P. Garrod and P. Greatorex respectively.
31. *CSPD* 19 February 1653, p.148; 29 April 1652, p.229; 15 March 1653, p.215.
32. Washbourn, Appendix XVIII, p.419.
33. GBR H2/3, ff.261–5 for 24 November 1657.
34. *CSPD* 4 January 1660, p.298, No.9.
35. Glos. Colln 10952 (30).
36. G.S. Blakeway, *The City of Gloucester ... and varying fortunes* (Gloucester, 1924), p.96.
37. GBR F4/5, ff.484–5.
38. Washbourn, p.clxxx.
39. GBR F4/5, f.242.
40. *Pers. comm.* Susanne Atkin, with thanks.

41. GBR F4/5, ff.395–6.
42. GBR F4/5, f.434.
43. GBR F4/5, ff.395–6.
44. GBR H2/3, f.67 for 20 August 1651.
45. The work cost £1,204–0–10d rather than the £50 estimated: CSPD July 1662, p.447.

CHAPTER 9. EFFECTS OF THE SIEGE AND THE CIVIL WAR

1. Clarendon II, p.475.
2. Dorney (1653), p.80.
3. C. Carlton, 'The impact of the fighting' in J. Morrill (ed.), *The Impact of the English Civil War* (London, 1991), p.17.
4. Foster, p. 261.
5. Washbourn, p. clviii.
6. Fosbrooke, p. 13.
7. Site 27/90: by M. Walters.
8. *A True Relation of the severall passages which have happened to our army since it advanced towards Gloucester with the manner of the relief of the same Sept. 14 1643.* British Library Thomason Tracts E58/23.
9. M. Holmes, 'Burials of Parliamentarians at Berkeley', *TBGAS* 73 (1953), pp.158–9.
10. S. Rudder, *New History of Gloucestershire* (Gloucester, 1779), p.172.
11. Corbet, p.61.
12. Corbet, p.25.
13. GBR B3/2, f.251 for 7 April 1643.
14. PRO SP 28 129/5, C13; C79.
15. GBR B3/2, f.376 for 3 July 1646.
16. PRO SP 28 129/5, C13; GBR G3/5O6, f.110 for 1657.
17. Letter of 24 November 1659 to Committee of Safety. Published in Washbourn, pp.430–1.
18. GBR B3/2, f.293 for 30 December 1643.
19. GBR G3/19.
20. Dorney (1653), pp. 20–1.
21. Washbourn, cxix.
22. HMC, p.507; GBR H2/3, ff.136–7.
23. *Presentation of the Grand Jury concerning Houses destroyed in the Siege,* quoted in Fosbrooke, pp.70–1.

24. Dorney (1653), p.21.

25. GBR J3/3, ff.205–6, 212–13, 223–8.

26. M. Atkin, 'Post-medieval archaeology in Gloucester: a review', *Post-Medieval Archaeology* 21 (1987), pp.12, 20–1.

27. S. Eward, *No Fine But a Glass of Wine* (Salisbury, 1985), p.160; GBR F4/5, f.273.

28. Rudder (note 8), p.172.

29. Petition to Parliament 1645 quoted in Washbourn, p.386.

30. GBR F4/5, f.273.

31. *Mercurius Aulicus*, 19 September.

32. GBR H2/3, f.35 for 30 November 1643.

33. PRO SP 28 129/5.

34. J.K.G. Taylor, 'The Civil Government of Gloucester, 1640–6', *TBGAS* 67 (1946), p.93.

35. *CSPD* August 1651, p.368; HMC, p.504.

36. Dorney (1653), p. 80.

37. W.H. Hoskins, *Local History in England* (London, 1959), p.177.

38. Groups of pre-Civil War pottery from the city are very similar to material from post-1660 dumps found on Lower Quay Street in 1979 (*pers. comm.* Alan Vince).

39. I.C. Walker, *Clay tobacco-pipes, with particular reference to the Bristol industry* (Parks Canada, 1977), p.686; S. Atkin, 'Clay tobacco pipes in Gloucester', *Glevensis* 22 (1988), p.43.

40. *CSPD* 30 June 1654, p.229.

41. *CSPD* 31 July 1654, pp.104–5.

42. C.M. MacInnes, *The Early English Tobacco Trade* (London, 1926), p.103.

43. PRO D621: E2, published in H.P.R. Finberg (ed.), *Gloucestershire Studies* (Leicester, 1957), pp.184–9.

44. N. Kingsley, *The Country Houses of Gloucestershire* (Cheltenham, 1989), p.8.

45. Washbourn, note 192.

46. H.P.R. Finberg, *op.cit.*, p.186; Clarendon II, p.512.

47. Letter of the Marquis of Worcester to Charles II, 1666–7. MSS of the Duke of Beaufort in HMC, p.60.

48. Dorney (1653), p. 4.

49. *Mercurius Rusticus; or the Countries Complaint* (London, 1685), quoted in GNQ 3 (1887), pp.136–7.

50. Ibid., pp.146–8.

Chapter 10. Conclusion

1. Clarendon, p.516.
2. Information from Phil Moss, a descendant of the original finder.
3. Dorney (1653), p.23.
4. C. Carlton, 'The impact of the fighting' in J. Morrill (ed.), *The Impact of the English Civil War* (London, 1991), p.30.
5. GBR B3/3, f.503 for 2 August 1672.

Appendix 2

1. Dorney, p.212.
2. Dorney, p.213.
3. Dorney, p.215.
4. *CSPD* 1641–3, 25 August 1643 No.151, p.479.
5. *CSPD* 1641–3, 21 August 1643 No.150, p.479.
6. Clarendon II, p.470.
7. J. Roland Phillips, *Civil War in Wales and the Marches* (London, 1874), p.211.
8. *Mercurius Civicus*. London's Intelligencer No.63, 1–8 August 1643. British Library Thomason Tracts E4.
9. Corbet, p.40.
10. Corbet, p.60.
11. Corbet, p.62.
12. HMC 14th Report, Duke of Portland MSS vol.III, Appendix II (HMSO, 1894), p.136.
13. *CSPD* 1644–5, 18 October 1644, pp.52–4.
14. Ibid., 12 February 1645, pp.301–2.
15. *CSPD* 1644–5, pp.266–8.
16. HMC 14th Report (see note 12).
17. Quoted in S. Lee (ed.), *Dictionary of National Biography*, vol. xxxvii, p.3.
18. Letter of Richard Watson to William Edgman, 7 September 1649, pubished in Washbourn, p.433
19. Clarendon III, p.616.
20. Clarendon State Papers III (1767), p.464.

Appendix 3

1. An extract from GBR F4/5, ff.179–194 in Gloucestershire Records Office. Transcribed by Barbara Drake, with thanks.

Index

Numbers in italics refer to illustrations. Appendices 1 and 3 have not been indexed.